SECOND CHANCES

SECOND CHANCES

by
Martha B. Hopkins

A.D. MM
FITHIAN PRESS
SANTA BARBARA, CALIFORNIA

Published by Fithian Press
A division of Daniel and Daniel, Publishers, Inc.
Post Office Box 1525
Santa Barbara, CA 93102

LIBRARY OF CONGRESS CATALOGING-IN-PUBLICATION DATA
Hopkins, Martha B., 1929–
    Second chances / by Martha B. Hopkins.
        p.   cm.
    ISBN 1-56474-316-0
    1. Africa, Southern—Description and travel.   2. Africa, Southern—
Social conditions—1975–   3. Hopkins, Martha B., 1929–   —Journeys—
Africa, Southern.   I. Title.
DT1036.H66   2000
968.06—dc21   99-27134
                                                   CIP

CONTENTS

PREFACE

Among the first events in the local news when I arrived back in Tucson was the bulldozing of a squatter's village, a shanty town erected by some homeless people. Pictures of California gang members voluntarily lining up at a medical clinic to have tattoos removed were on the front page.

After five months in southern Africa, I had returned with a big dent in my head from a bloody car wreck, rife with recollections of shanty towns and tattooed gang members, and an incredible sequence of unanticipated experiences during their spring and summer of 1995–1996.

Apartheid and the "old South Africa" had ended less than six years earlier. Nelson Mandela had been president for less than two years and the "new South Africa" was still forming. So much hope and reconciliation, so much energy, so much building and progress. And so much greed and violence, despair and intrigue. So many tribal, cultural, ethnic and petty rivalries.

I was privileged to watch parliamentary debates on the new South African Constitution—which already included many things that we have been struggling to add to ours for 200 years. And I had a fascinating private meeting with the speaker of the Namibian Parliament.

I visited several townships, including Soweto, with a black man who ten years ago could easily have been detained and tortured in the very police station, turned pizza parlor, where we had lunch. In another township the first trumpet player of the

Cape Town Symphony was teaching small black kids to play brass instruments.

I was with a handsome young black couple on their very first stay in a hotel, a story with several peculiar twists.

Experiences like becoming the "Auntie" on remote sheep farms in the Great Karoo, watching almost every African wild animal, witnessing the birth of a butterfly and having inadvertently been on the edge of a counterfeiting and diamond-smuggling scam in Namibia just kept happening. I attended the autopsies of a murdered white woman, a dehydrated black baby, an assassinated coloured gang member and a man who had been burned to death in a shantytown fire.

I had been a print writer for years but decided to begin writing for radio. One of my first pieces was a half-hour program on the emerging ratite industry in Arizona—ostriches, etc., as food, leather, feathers, oil and maybe veins and corneas for transplant to people. I met a number of South Africans in the process, which intensified my interest in the area. The expiration of my lease and a small legacy from a recently deceased elderly aunt clinched the trip.

I told my friend Sam Taylor, one of the best blues musicians in the country, that I was going to South Africa. His eyes lit up and the stocky ex-boxer and elegant musician said, "I want to go." So I had another mission: help get this black man to Africa.

The scenery in southern Africa is surprisingly varied and unfailingly beautiful. Some people might not find Namibia or the Karoo wonderful, but I am fundamentally a desert person, despite the fact that I have lived in and love a number of cities from coast to coast in the States—"America," as the Africans commonly refer to my homeland.

On my first day in Cape Town, I wrote in my laptop notes: "This is sort of a forty-year regression for me—San Francisco, mountains, ocean, fog and brilliance and falling in love." I'm one of those people who are always in love. More of that later. Unedited notes from my laptop computer head several chapters and are occasionally included in the present text.

Mixed in with encountering different cultures and customs and a whole suite of new experiences, I was developing a sense, a real sense, of the history of my own country. And I began to realize that at another level I was reliving earlier experiences in my life, with the rare chance to do things right the second time around. Comparisons with what I knew of my country and what I was learning were inevitable and are interspersed throughout.

Some of the countries in southern Africa also are getting a second chance to do things right; my experiences in South Africa and Namibia have taught me much about them and me. That's what this book is about—second chances.

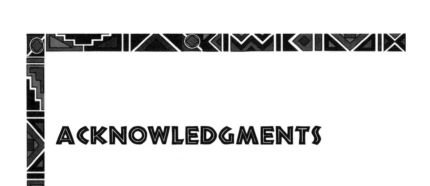

ACKNOWLEDGMENTS

James Baran is the kind of friend that everyone needs—a person who speaks the truth.

Tom and Ronnelle de Villiers shared their relatives, friends, and experiences.

Lisa Bowden helped with the computer part.

Wendy and Chris Benner already know much of what I am talking about and are careful editors.

Sally Benson is always looking for the "good flow," and over the years has been a wonderfully constructive critic.

Deon Knobel edited parts of the chapter on the autopsies and made so many things possible in the first place.

Alison Deming, more than most people, understands the role of words and the edges of the civilized world.

Brian Laird gave his thoughtful editing, general encouragement, and the remarkable suggestions about moving sections around.

And to my publisher, John Daniel, who upon my first return from Africa said, "You've got to write a book."

Thanks to all of the people in southern Africa who extended themselves mightily to make this record so rich.

TUCSON, ARIZONA
MAY 1999

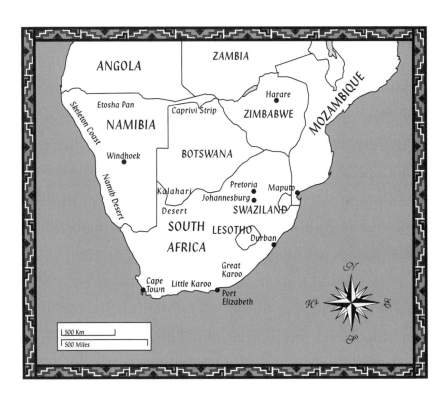

ANGOLA

ZAMBIA

Skeleton Coast

Etosha Pan

NAMIBIA

Caprivi Strip

ZIMBABWE

Harare

MOZAMBIQUE

Windhoek

BOTSWANA

Namib Desert

Kalahari
Desert

Pretoria

Johannesburg

Maputo

SWAZILAND

SOUTH
AFRICA

LESOTHO

Durban

Great
Karoo

Cape
Town

Little Karoo

Port
Elizabeth

N

W

E

S

500 Km

500 Miles

SECOND CHANCES

CHAPTER 1

BLOOD AND
THE FIRST HOTEL

I'm grateful for a lovely day—more interesting than love-ly, and thanks be for Solly and Lena not being hurt. And also thanks for my life and not maiming me and not hurt-ing my computer.

Dec. 23, 1996, 6:15 P.M., town of Warden

I was scheduled to join a three-day Christmas holiday tour to Durban leaving from Pretoria. At the last minute the trip was canceled because a party of four had backed out. The travel agent informed the three of us remaining that our reservations at the Holiday Inn would be held until the next morning; so the young black couple and I began to talk.

I had never met them before, but intuition on first encounters is valuable if you trust yourself. They were both in their mid-twenties, attractive, articulate, pleasant. Both had jobs and were very open talking about money and expense sharing. Neither Solly nor Lena had a driver's license.

I was the Anglo with the gray hair, the driver's license and the credit card, so I could rent a car and we could drive to the coastal resort for Christmas as planned. After much shuffling of papers to figure out refunds from the agent, to calculate gas, rental fees and other costs, we decided to go for it.

Not only was it the Christmas holidays, it was midsummer. Johannesburg, Pretoria and other major cities emptied out for much of December. Those who could usually headed for the numerous southern coastal resorts in and around Durban on

17

the Indian Ocean, or Cape Town on the Atlantic coast of South Africa. Last-minute hotel reservations were impossible to get, but with that base covered, and with someone to share expenses, I headed for Avis to rent a car.

After several hours that night of practicing driving "on the other side," parking and familiarizing myself with the South African model of a Toyota Corolla, I packed and went to bed in anticipation of a long day driving the 500 kilometers.

We met very early the next morning and immediately, as agreed, they gave me half of their share of the anticipated costs, the other half to be paid upon our return.

I noticed that without discussion Lena automatically got in the back seat. Convention, I guessed. I handed Solly the Automobile Association maps (the AA is the equivalent of our AAA) and asked him to help navigate out of town and find the road to Durban in the maze of freeway exits.

Many people are not good at reading maps, but shortly it was clear that this young man had little experience at it. He was embarrassed (or whatever) to admit errors, which began to pile up. Nothing fatal, but after several disconcerting instructions like "turn here, no don't turn here," we were out of Pretoria, on our merry way along with hundreds of other cars, two days before Christmas.

Most of the road to Durban was freeway, some of it toll road, and while the weather was overcast and threatening, conditions were dry and clear. The nine-year drought had been broken with a vengeance during the last few weeks in KwaZulu Natal and in the eastern part of the Free State, which we were traversing. Creeks were high, and signs of flooding were everywhere.

As almost everywhere in South Africa, the scenery was pleasing. We climbed gradually to the high veld, rich corn-and-cotton-producing areas with lovely rolling hills completely checkered with large beige recently harvested fields. In the far distance ahead stood the spectacular Drakensburg mountains.

The roads were straight, and the pace picked up even though the maximum speed limit was 120 kilometers per hour (about 65 miles per hour). Sprinkled among the numerous sedans were the ever-present minibus taxis, called combis, packed to the seams with black people. Not many black people in South

Africa yet owned cars, and combis were the main method of motor transportation. Needless to say, when there was an accident, it was horrendous because of the overcrowding.

We chatted about many things. Surprisingly to me, Solly and Lena had never been to Durban, and even more surprising was that they had never stayed in a hotel—mainly a result of apartheid, travel and other restrictions, to say nothing of little money. I constantly needed to filter my observations of black people experiencing new things for the first time with the realization that it had been a mere six years since the formal death of apartheid, and the new Constitution was still being drafted. Obvious racism was still abundant everywhere, but ten years ago this young couple was poor, segregated and, the man in particular, in ever-present danger of terrible abuse.

The much-discussed phenomenon of highways full of speeding Mercedes and BMWs became disconcertingly evident. With recurrent frequency one or the other would shoot by us as though we were standing still. Every few miles we began to see a stalled or disabled car—never a BMW or Mercedes—and occasionally a combi. The residue of car accidents began to appear, with rarely a cop in sight.

Here and there the road conditions or the terrain would change, and the flow of traffic would suddenly thicken. Fortunately the two northbound lanes were separated from the two southbound by a grassy ditch. I'm a very defensive driver and try to leave at least a couple of car lengths' space between me and the car ahead; but the gap ahead often would be quickly filled with a darting BMW or big Mercedes and, frighteningly, sometimes by a loaded combi. Our car didn't have cruise control, but I diligently obeyed the speed limit, not wanting to be cited in a foreign country. And I kept in the far left lane next to the shoulder, the slow lane.

We chatted more and decided to stop at the historic old Harrismith Hotel for lunch. But it would be a while until we got there because my "navigator" paid more attention to the scenery than to the signs and maps. He told me to turn at the next road, which would take us to Durban—by way of Ladysmith. I had caught a sign out of the corner of my eye and had an uneasy feeling that something was incorrect; but I was fond of the Ladysmith Black Mambazo musicians, so we took what turned out to be a time-consuming detour. Fields were flooded, and streams were about to flow over the road, so I was glad to eventually get back on the main road, even without seeing much of Ladysmith.

The driving had been a "piece of cake" so far; but then without warning—no sound, no bump, nothing—the rear end fishtailed quickly to the left. Having driven on ice and snow, I knew how to maneuver. But, to my horror, the correction led to a fishtailing in the opposite direction. I swerved between two cars and then out and around and back into the same lane. The uncontrollable swerving continued, and as I made my last correction from the right lane to get back to the left, the car gradually rolled over. My quadrant was the first to hit, and I have a distinct memory of a minute or so of scraping, screeching, shattering sounds as we skidded straight down the freeway upside down.

All was very quiet when I woke up. A sensuous feeling of warm, flowing fluid was bathing me, but when I opened my eyes, my eyeglasses still on and undamaged, I realized that we were upside down, hanging in the seat belts, and that the fluid puddling on the "floor" was my blood. I asked Solly if he was okay. He said yes. Lena too. I told him to reach over and push my seat belt release. I plopped a short distance into the pool of glass chips and blood, with little room to spare because the top of the car was crunched in to just a little bit larger than my head. I climbed under Solly and pushed him up so that I could release his belt. Lena had extricated herself, so the three of us crawled out the broken window on the passenger side.

They were spattered with blood, my blood, but I was drenched, hair, clothes, shoes. A small cluster of people was there as we wriggled out, including a nearly hysterical woman who kept jumping up and down saying, "I saw the whole thing...the tire came off." Everyone kept saying, "You're so lucky."

A mountain of a man stepped forward and in a deep bass voice said, "I am a doctor. You are a very lucky person." I told him to look at the kids first. Solly had a small cut on his toe (it was hot and he had on sandals), and Lena was shaken but uninjured. I was a bloody mess but wasn't aware of any injury except to my head. The crowd grew, and six strong guys turned the car right side up. I laughed when I saw all the maps stuck to the ceiling with my blood. Others didn't seem to think it was so funny.

My bleeding had slowed down because the doctor had folded a cloth and ordered me to press it tight on the wound. Eventually two cops and an ambulance showed up, and we were helped into the back. We drove slowly for what seemed like a long time past the newly planted fields and then into Warden, a small town with one main street—a wide, dusty, dingy main street banded with a fringe of black people, spreading up and down from the door of a bottle store. Many were well on their way to being drunk in that awful, small-town-poverty-type drunk.

The doctor's office was in a modest home up a little hill just off a dirt road. It was crowded with people with varying degrees of visible and invisible problems, all ages, all black except me, the doctor, three assistants and the cop who stayed with us. Apparently I was a gruesome mess. I could tell by the way people flinched when they saw me. I tried to be pleasant and to say I was okay.

Soon we became the next on the triage list. After insisting that he first clear Solly and Lena, the young Afrikaner doctor, whose name I only remember as being pronounced like "Small," led me into his lab/examining/operating room. He looked at and probed my head gently and then meticulously cut the hair away from my wound with fingernail scissors. I was very impressed and told him that I had anticipated the customary treatment of an electric razor shave.

Anyone who has had kids knows how bloody scalp wounds are. But my pupils were the same size, I wasn't dizzy, and although my pulse was up, my blood pressure was fine; so I knew, and he was very relieved that I knew, that I was okay. "You're very lucky. Six people were killed in that stretch of road yesterday," he said. He dug several pieces of glass out of my head, cleaned me up, gave me a packet of gauze patches to use as compresses and turned us over to the policeman, who drove us to the police station to give a report.

The police station was an ugly, plain little building

surrounded, like all others I had seen, with very high wire fencing topped with razor wire. Solly and Lena froze and asked if they had to go in. I said no. They walked away from the barbed-wire enclosure and waited by the side of the road.

Most of the white-shirted, white-skinned officers behind the counter clearly preferred Afrikaans to English, but I was assigned to a young man with reasonably good English who kept looking at me as though I were from another planet. Several sprigs of my gray hair stood up in blood-red points around the wound, and my uncombed bangs had turned pink from being wiped off. At least my face had been cleaned up, but my clothes were still drenched. He filled out the report in Afrikaans. When I asked for a copy, I definitely was nearly asking for the moon. The chief or some authoritarian figure came out and said I didn't need one; but I insisted and said I was glad to pay for it. After a long time he came back with a hot piece of paper that was very hard to read, apparently made on a primitive copying machine. No charge.

When I walked out, Solly and Lena were standing beside our devastated car. It was badly smashed in front, but luckily the trunk (the "boot") was not badly deformed, and to our relief, the luggage was unharmed. This was especially lucky for me because my laptop computer was in there. We walked across the street to the towing/wrecking shop. The wife of the owner was very concerned about me because of all the blood, but she also was clearly puzzled about what I was doing with two black people. (As in the U.S., farm communities tended to be rather conservative and not very imaginative.)

She said that there was only one hotel in town which was several blocks down on this one main street. I asked her to call and reserve two rooms, which she did, and with considerable compassion and concern she offered to have her husband get our luggage and drive us down there. I accepted with many thanks. Automatically my partners headed for the back seats.

The owner of the hotel was aghast at my appearance when she saw me, but friendly until she saw the black couple. Her face hardened. It became very easy to imagine her saying, "Get out of here, you scum." I stepped forward, glared right into her eyes and said "I want two rooms next to each other and here is 500 rand (about 150 dollars) on account." She knew I meant it. I do think it was the first time that black people had ever been guests in that hotel, but when she realized that it was inevitable, she again became concerned. She said that one of the maids could wash my clothes. I was very grateful to her because I had thought I would have to discard everything, including a new L.L. Bean broadcloth shirt.

After the three of us had unpacked and cleaned up we headed for the dining room. It now was mid-afternoon and we were starving. The help (all black) also were surprised by our grouping, and while the kids had never stayed overnight at a hotel, they had eaten out at some very nice restaurants in Pretoria. Their manners and composure made things more comfortable for everyone. A few minutes later, Solly began looking at me in a peculiar way. "What is it?" I asked. He put his finger on his forehead and said, "You're leaking." I wiped my forehead with the white cloth napkin, and it was covered with bright red blood.

I told them to stay in or just outside our rooms and not to roam around because there were too many drunken people of all colors around. They understood. I first had to call Avis in Pretoria. They said they would have another car to us by 9:30 that night.

The cocktail waitress walked me back over to the doctor's office again. He really looked weary, but we talked more as he cleaned me up again and gently tweezed out newly discovered pieces of glass. When I declined to have a huge compression bandage covering my whole head, he put in a stitch and said we'd try it my way this time, but if it broke open again, I should have the bandage.

I commented that he looked so tired. He was. There had been a steady stream of people for several days, and the worst was yet to come. I asked him what a nice guy like him was doing in a place like that. He laughed and said yes, the pay was low and the hours long, but he liked being in a place where people really needed the help. A good country doctor! He only wished that he had another doctor or medical assistant and more help. A bell rang, indicating his front door had been opened. He sighed and said, "next patient." The helpers had left promptly at five o'clock, so we both headed for the front door. I was not prepared to see a man almost as bloody as I had been, but it looked like the lower part of his arm was hanging on by a thread. A thoroughly distraught woman and a solemn man held him up. The waitress and I left.

We wouldn't have a car until 9:30 that night and it had started to rain hard, so we agreed to stay overnight and head for Durban early in the morning. I had a good TV in my room, the kids had one that didn't work, so I suggested that we exchange rooms and told them not to open the door for anyone except me. I taught them a special knock that had been my telephone buzz signal in college.

My head was very tender, but I knew that I was just shaken up and should rest until the car came and then get a good night's sleep. I was almost asleep when a loud, rude knock came on my door. It had to be the kids, so I jumped up and opened the door. To our mutual surprise, it was a huge blond guy I had seen in the bar, already well on his way to being drunk two hours ago. He sputtered but said nothing and quickly turned and disappeared down the hall. To this day I wonder what his plan was.

To my astonishment, the maid had gotten my shirt snow-white, so I put it on with a clean skirt. The sky was still cloudy, but the rain had let up, so we had breakfast in the dining room and left for Durban. Flooded fields and ditches were everywhere. We all looked for the place where our accident occurred and thought we found it, except that there were so many skid marks we couldn't tell which were ours.

We passed by Pietermaritsburg. I had told Solly and Lena earlier about the Church of the Covenant, which the Boers had erected after defeating the Zulu at the famous battle of Blood River. Originally we had planned to visit it but decided to skip it.

Durban is a large and intricate city on the shores of the usually balmy Indian Ocean. My passenger's map-reading skills just weren't up to helping find the Holiday Inn South, especially since this was their first time there. So we parked and together devised a route.

It was windy and cold, with on and off rain, a real-vacation wrecker for those who expected to spend their holiday getting tan on the glorious beaches. It was an unusual and undesired weather system that perhaps only a few weather people understood—I had heard that it had something to do with La Niña, which is a cold ocean current, the opposite of El Niño.

I slept most of December 24 and canceled my arrangements with music friends from Cape Town to "do the town" for a couple of days. Very disappointing, because Durban is an historic, incredibly sophisticated and varied town, musically and otherwise.

I also canceled any thought of calling or visiting Die Lewende Testament Vereniging, the Afrikaans translation of the Living Will Society. I had heard brief mention of the group on a radio program in Cape Town, but no one with whom I spoke seemed to know anything about it—but they liked the idea of having a living will. The knowledge of and fascination with the subject of having a say in one's own death was about the same as it had been in the U.S. ten years ago, when I wrote several stories about the rise of the movement.

On the top of my clothes in a suitcase was my own living will, which spelled out very specifically my wishes regarding my own life and death, what I did and didn't want in terms of "heroic measures" and who my designated "plug puller" was. I'm not sure what validity it would have had in South Africa, and I'm not even sure of the legal aspects of the phrase that I had added to my formal document—instructing my executor to sue any nurse, doctor, hospital or anyone who violated my rights and wishes about the ending of my own life.

I ordered room service, lay in bed healing and occasionally got up and looked out at Natal Bay and observed an ever-growing plume of tan silt being fed into the slate-gray waters by the major rivers draining into it. Clearly there was big-time flooding upstream. Once I walked down the hall to where I could see a raging storm over the Indian Ocean. Rarely, even in Tucson, had I ever seen such lightning. Here and there I saw a foolish bather on the beach, and hundreds, if not thousands, of tightly secured little spikes of folded umbrellas standing on the beach.

"Dr. Small" had given me some special antiseptic shampoo, but I wasn't supposed to get my head wet for a few more days, so I still had the stiff bloody peaks and pink bangs; they were startling to see when I glanced in the mirror. On Christmas Day, I lay around taking aspirin watching the *Sound of Music* and news of disastrous flooding with bloated bodies floating down raging rivers that had been dry for the last nine years.

I reflected on other Christmases, especially one twenty years ago when I stayed at a beachfront hotel on the shores of the Pacific Ocean in Santa Monica, California, during a dreadful divorce. Things were a thousand percent better now, despite the car accident. It seemed that I would have a hell of a dent in my head forever, but fortunately it was just beyond the hair line, so nothing showed.

An Afrikaner I later met gleefully told me about a black woman on a farm who had a very abusive husband. He knocked her down and threw a huge rock down on her head. "It would have killed a white person, but you know how thick their skulls are," I was told. The black woman was up and around and a few days later only had a small bruise. After my own collisions with the windshield, the steel brace and the freeway with only a dent to show for them, I was not sure what that made me.

CHAPTER 2

BIRTH, LIFE AND SOME DEATH

The way things are unfolding, it seems that I need to re-live parts of my life in order to understand. Where is all this leading? A period of revelation for me. How can I capture it? How can I make all of my good fortune translate into really useful stuff?

From week two, Cape Town

Just north of the much-travelled and scenically wonderful "Garden Route" on the southern tip of the African continent are parallel ranges of semi-arid mountains: the Little Karoo and, north of it, the vast Great Karoo.

Oudtshoorn (more or less pronounced oats'-horn), in the heart of the great Karoo, is the ostrich capital of the world. While ostrich meat (a delicate red meat resembling beef) is widely eaten in southern Africa, one of the biggest industries is exporting fertile eggs and breeding pairs to other countries all over the world to initiate ostrich industries there. Great Britain has a much different climate, but successful ostrich raising was increasing there when mad-cow disease struck. Mad-cow quickly wrecked the British beef industry, but British Airways promptly began serving ostrich fillets to its first class passengers. Let's hope a "mad ostrich disease" doesn't develop. They're mean enough as is, can run forty miles per hour, tear the door off a truck, kill a person with one kick and, as one grower put it, "are not blessed with great intelligence."

Ostriches are, in fact, a big deal in South Africa. Their three-toed feet are much more gentle on the delicate deserts than either sheep or the heavy hooves of cattle. Ostriches are valuable primarily for meat, leather, feathers and potential uses of other parts, like transplanting ostrich corneas and veins to humans. The large ostrich cooperative, with facilities for slaughter and processing, making biltong (jerky), museum displays, feather merchants, leather crafting, fertile and decorative ostrich eggs and related industries are major elements of the economy in Oudtshoorn.

It's an old, historic and very Afrikaans part of the country, the crossroads for large and sparsely populated areas to the east, north and west. Major downtown hotels in Oudtshoorn and the Old Feather Inn in mid-town are enjoying top-to-bottom restoration, including elegant displays in sealed glass cases of incredible ostrich feathers, some of which are snow-white and appear to be over three feet long.

The solitude and beauty of the Karoo and Oudtshoorn's proximity to the Garden Route, the Klein Karoo wine district, the ostriches and other attractions make this town an important tourist destination as well as a commercial hub. Tourist-oriented ostrich farms, ostrich races, ostrich product gift shops and other attractions like the Cango Caves have existed for a long while. (In some literature and maps Cango is spelled Kango, originally a Bushman word.)

A large alligator breeding park and a facility where you can literally pet the cheetahs are close to town. On a well-established ostrich farm near the limestone caves, the owner, Mr. Danie Lategan, had the wisdom to give a woman artist and scientific illustrator, Jill Reid, some space on which to establish a butterfly farm. There are a few other butterfly farms in the world, most with the same purpose of helping species that have been threatened by development, drought or disease to survive by breeding and release.

The Cango Butterfly Farm, the newest and smallest attraction in the area, has a number of interesting butterfly and moth displays—front and back, boy and girl, mature and immature etc., and it has several "birthing" rooms. For me it was one of the most fascinating places I had ever been.

At the Old Feather Inn, where I was staying, after much fuss-

ing I hung over the front desk counter as the clerk held one end
of a connecting wire into the office telephone and typed the following e-mail message to my friend Alison Deming, director of
the University of Arizona Poetry Center:

> Can hardly contain myself with over-joy. Just came from
> the Cango Butterfly Farm; while I was watching a half-
> hour-old African monarch dry its wings, another but-
> terfly was born before my very eyes.
> It broke the shell of the chrysalis, and I heard the
> crack. The top half and then the bottom half fell silent-
> ly on the dirt floor. A tight, compact yellow ball with a
> long black sac of fluid on the bottom was carefully hold-
> ing onto the twig with one tiny black leg, and then an-
> other leg unfolded.
> Gradually it pumped up its beautiful wings with the
> fluid, and then the sac fell off as it gently exercised its
> wings to dry them. "A healthy little girl," announced Jill
> Reid, the founder of the haven. Three spots instead of
> four.
> Jill raises them by providing the necessary food and
> environment and then folds each one up and puts it in
> an envelope to be driven to places as far as seven hours
> away to be released into the wild.
> Am having my first taste of Witzblitz, probably 100
> proof, a local farm concoction that undoubtedly con-
> tributes to butterfly power. Told her about your book....

Alison, a prominent American writer, had just finished a book of
poetry and essays called *The Monarchs*. But my God, who
wouldn't be fascinated by this miracle of nature...a perfect
birth. Farm kids and a fortunate few others have witnessed this
particular event, but not me, and I was mightily affected.

In the adjacent room filled with tall moist plants, ferns and
vines, we found a beautiful large, pale-blue newborn butterfly
floating lifeless on the surface of a little pond. Drowned. A doz-
en others flitted around the edge of the pond as though they
were concerned.

Life and death occur so differently in cities. I had been in

Africa quite a while and had read about, heard about and witnessed so much of life and death. The culling of this butterfly,
for whatever reason, seemed less violent than a gunshot wound
to the head. While nature can be fierce, it is impersonal.

The night before this wonderful day of birth I saw on the
television news a young boy in a casket who had been murdered
in a gang fight. Gangs were numerous and big in South Africa,
and now that the country had been targeted by organized crime
as a lucrative drug market, things were getting worse. The boy's
sobbing mother and relatives circulated around the small body
in a satin box in a way that reminded me of the butterflies flut-
tering around the edge of the pond. Death and life in the new
South Africa.

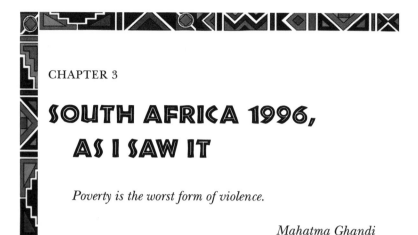

CHAPTER 3

SOUTH AFRICA 1996, AS I SAW IT

Poverty is the worst form of violence.

Mahatma Ghandi

The "new" South Africa, as it is referred to reverentially by those who are grateful for a second chance, is a term invoked scornfully by others.

A wide variety of reasons are given for their disdain, ranging from potholes, late busses, incompetent labor and the arrogance of newly appointed well-paid civil servants, to statements like, "I get along with blacks and coloureds but things were fine the way they were," or "I'm not a racist, but...the blacks are destroying what used to be wonderful farmland because they don't know what they are doing." Others say "I pay fifty percent of my hard-earned salary to support those lazy people." "They have taken away our beautiful old flag and replaced it with that new thing." Scoffing at the new South Africa is convenient for anything that needs to be explained away, including personal failures, uncertainty, fear and ignorance.

While huge problems face the totally revised nation that came into existence on April 27, 1994, among my reasons for being optimistic about the future, notwithstanding a violent past, is an attitude that I found astonishing to behold: the quest for reconciliation is more powerful than the thirst for vengeance of the majority. This does not mean forgetting or overlooking crimes on all sides, but there is a patent awareness that "tit for tat" leads sideways or downward, not forward.

Fortunately much of the world seems to recognize Nelson Mandela as a rare man whose timing has been fortuitously perfect. For being so gentle, he is amazingly tough. Because I was on the scene, I could hear the whole of his speeches and be filled in on surrounding circumstances.

One evening I turned on the TV at a critical moment when Mandela was being interviewed by some black newscaster. I had never seen him so unsmiling, uncompromising and resolutely clear. He had just invited Castro and Khadahfe to South Africa and apparently had taken some flak from various countries, including the U.S. He looked straight into the camera and said "the West's enemies are not my enemies. These are the people who stayed with us. No one will tell me who my friends are." That element of not forgetting who your true friends are increased my admiration even more.

I arrived in October, the South African spring, as the new Constitution was being debated and revised. Vigorous effort was expended on television and radio to teach people how the government of the new South Africa worked—the mechanics, like how to mark a ballot. Illiteracy was still rampant, especially in people of color, any color; so in elections the ballots had, in addition to the candidate's names, pictures of the candidates and the party colors for those who couldn't read. The preponderance of people were voting for their local officials for the first time in history.

The enthusiasm for teaching people how to do things and for understanding why voting and helping shape one's government is important, reminded me of the private Nairobi School in East Palo Alto, California. East Palo Alto was a poor black ghetto just east of a freeway that separated it from affluent and "liberal" Palo Alto, home of Stanford University. In the late fifties and sixties, with the rise of "black power," civil rights awareness and desegregation decisions that would lead to busing school children to achieve integration, a woman named Gertrude Wilks said "Stop." "Our [black] children can learn. Give us the money, and we will teach them. Filling yellow buses with little black faces and taking them out of their neighborhoods to hostile environments is wrong."

Wilks had gone along with what parents of school-age

children were supposed to do in those days—made sure her kids were on time, attend conferences and parent-teacher association meetings and the like.

On graduation day her oldest son came to her and said "Mama, I can't read." (It was not an uncommon practice in those days to just pass a student on to the next grade just to get rid of him.) Soon he was in prison, and she vowed that that would not happen to her other children. She was a strong advocate of the now much-discussed subject of providing vouchers so that black children could be taught by black teachers in black schools near their homes. The white school board and the superintendent, whom I personally know to be petty and bigoted, accused her of being racist and basically unpatriotic. But she persisted against all odds.

A number of white people, including me, tried to assist the private school she had founded through fund raising and other activities. Criticism from both blacks and whites was rampant. The school was frequently vandalized and twice burned down. Defiantly, classes were held outdoors. It was a painful period in the history of my county, but perhaps a necessary step.

Much of my early understanding of that which is truly African came from Gertrude Wilks. I was permitted to attend some events that were almost exclusively black and was forever affected by the singing and drums. But Gertrude often reminded me that the biggest job of education was to be done on my side of the freeway.

A note on the term coloured (now called mixed-race people): Around the year 1800 there were about 20,000 white Europeans in Cape Town, about that many slaves, mainly from India and the Far East, and about 15,000 Hottentots (black herdsmen), who were among those who welcomed Jan Van Riebeck, the Dutch explorer who came to South Africa in 1652. Van Riebeck's principal purpose was to promote the interests of the VOC, the Dutch East India Company. Soon thereafter, the Hottentots were more than decimated by the "white man's disease," smallpox.

Despite every effort to keep the races separate, they soon were intermingled, producing a mulatto group with skin color ranging from light to dark brown. Usually facial features were more European than negroid, and to this day these usually very handsome people are known as "coloured"...with a "u."

In his autobiography, Mandela has a lot to say about coloureds and other groups. In prisons, whites get more and better food than Indians or coloureds, and blacks get the least and the worst—part of the usual pecking order.

Various nationalities of Asian peoples, including Indians (from India) and other racial and religious groups, still live together—by choice—in distinct neighborhoods in the "new South Africa." My flat in Cape Town, the "Mother City," as it is known, was in a mostly white neighborhood in Tamboeskloof, not far from the Malay Quarter. If the atmospheric conditions were just right, I could hear the Muslim call to prayer from the numerous mosques; and the prayers were broadcast in full over a Muslim radio station—a solemn and lovely experience for me. When I lived in Washington, D.C., I watched a beautiful mosque being built from the ground up. The interior mosaic and tile work in some mosques was incredibly intricate and detailed, but sometimes poorly lighted.

Differences in past expenditure of public monies between blacks and whites in South Africa were desperately clear in the townships. I visited several township schools, including one near Cape Town that was literally falling down. There was nothing on the walls of the narrow halls: no maps, no pictures, no charts, no messages, nothing. Nothing on the principal's dilapidated desk but an old telephone and a few papers: no staplers, no Post-It notes, no in/out box or marble-based pen sets. While listening to the principal explain his hopes for a new building, I shifted my weight and my foot went through the floor. He apologized profusely (like it was his fault!) and then said, "If you're going to be in this country and truly understand, you need to know how to do this." He taught me an "African handshake." (One clasps the other's right hand in a conventional handshake then, each slides his hand up and grasps the other person's thumb, then the hands slide back down to another conventional handshake.)

I was fortunate to be able to visit parts of a number of townships under differing circumstances. Some experiences contributed to my immense optimism about a healthy future for South

Africa: In a township near Cape Town, a fine new community center, where elderly folks could have a hot free lunch and social interaction, had been built by the residents. A "medical" center had been built in a clean, simple new building, ill-stocked and ill-equipped, but the first of its kind for miles around. A woman, possibly illiterate and unhealthy herself, is selected from each neighborhood in the township (many townships have tens or hundreds of thousands of people; Soweto has over three million) to be trained in such things as basic hygiene, how pregnancy occurs (still a mystery to some young mothers), family planning, food groups, nutrition and first aid and disease prevention. Those trained make regular visits to their neighbors and teach other women what they have learned. It works, in part, because of the ongoing support of dedicated government workers and volunteers, including the Students' Health and Welfare Centres Organisation (SHAWCO). This organization, which has existed for over fifty years, is a group of medical students from the University of Cape Town who over the years have established trust in the townships and, even though still students, they render invaluable service in townships with the aid of regular doctors, mobile clinics, and public support.

I visited Khayelitsha with some students in their old van, which had SHAWCO clearly painted on the doors, front and back. Residents waved, and the students waved back as they drove through townships to assist at whatever medical facilities existed. Clearly the van was recognized and accepted. One of the students very matter of factly said, "Don't drive through here on your own."

The memory of other experiences, however, leaves me with a turned stomach: acres, if not square miles, of dusty, filthy shacks with no running water or toilets; tiny starved children with swollen bellies so tight that when a doctor gently thumped them, they sounded like drums; the children's blank, unchanging expression; black children whose black hair has turned golden yellow because of severe protein and other deficiencies, suffering from diminished mental abilities due to malnutrition; listless young people with running sores; and pregnant young teenage girls with four stair-step kids unsmilingly following them.

Outside one place where we stopped was a community

"radio station" in an old trailer, which broadcast a signal just strong enough to reach a small area. When the few publicly owned radios had batteries to receive (or when a radio was freshly stolen) the residents could receive health, nutrition and AIDS information and other survival tips. And the station gave people a chance to voice their opinions and be heard—a vital element in mental health.

During my five-month stay, the draft of the Constitution for the new South Africa was completed, circulated and discussed, but not ratified until May, after I had returned to the U.S. A huge problem that remained unresolved, even with the ratification of the new Constitution, was the legitimate interests of two militant minority parties, one black, the Inkatha Freedom party, and one white, the former rulers of the apartheid era, the National Party.

The ruling coalition of the African National Congress party, led by Nelson Mandela, and the National Party lasted for two years, until F.W. de Klerk's conservatives split off to form a second party. It was probably a healthy thing for the fledgling democracy to have at least two strong parties.

The ongoing struggle between the ruling ANC and Inkatha, the dominant party in the province of KwaZulu-Natal, had led to much bloodshed over the years. Inkatha, fearing that the more centralized government promulgated by the ANC would destroy Zulu culture and dilute provincial authority, had boycotted the constitutional process and passed its own provincial constitution. In the U.S. we have the same type of conflict, but here it's called states rights vs. the federal government. Fortunately most of the killing over the subject ended with the end of our Civil War in 1865; but to this day there is a war of words in the U.S.

In September 1996, the Constitutional Court, the highest court in South Africa, rejected both the national and provincial constitutions, thus permitting the redrawing of a federal constitution that would include more provincial powers. It beats killing. This ability to "work things out by process" is part of why I remain optimistic about South Africa's future.

When President Mandela, legislatures and courts strive for economic and social equity, a few still shout "communist." That doesn't work anymore because it's not true, and people know that it's not. Some socialist elements, maybe; communist, no; and fiercely capitalistic in many quarters. There will be redistribution of wealth at some levels, but much of the existing wealth has come from the sweat and blood and property of others who now want their land back and a fair shot at prospering. For example, a tribal authority has claimed back-title to some land in Kruger Park, from which they were removed at gunpoint in 1969. They don't plan to take back the land physically, but having the title would allow them to operate and share in the profits of ecotourism.

Another splendid example is a highly successful fruit-farming cooperation in the north between formerly rigid Boer farmers and formerly angry black people who now have land ownership. Together they produce abundant export-grade agricultural products.

Getting on with life now that economic sanctions have been lifted has resulted in many other new economic and social activities, and—thrilling to observe—self-esteem at all levels of society.

Sports are a big deal in South Africa. The country hosted a huge multinational rugby tournament in 1995—and won. Their newly renamed soccer team, Bafana Bafana, then defeated Tunisia in the Africa Cup. The 1996 Olympic games in Atlanta continued to foster South Africa's pride in its athletes, black and white, who won several gold and other medals. Subsequent correspondence with friends in South Africa confirmed what some of us here thought—the Olympic coverage was lopsidedly red-white-blue and terribly commercial. I rarely get pumped up about a collegiate match, let alone the NFL, so I was surprised by the gladness and pride I felt when watching some of the sporting events. Yay team!

And South Africa won several cricket test matches and an international cricket match—which is so "very British." Black youth are now playing cricket on formerly "white only" teams, and some of them are good. But only one South African big leaguer exists right now. To me, cricket is God's most mysterious game.

Some of those cricket games take *five* days. At the risk of never having my South African visa renewed, I will say that to the casual observer like me, a cricket game looks like a guy with a flat paddle and a helmet and pads all over standing in front of three sticks stuck vertically in the ground with a fourth one balanced across the top. Another guy with no hat on called the bowler, comes running at top speed down a grassy field and with a straight arm makes a three-quarter swing back over his head, close to his ear, and throws—bowls—a small hard ball as fast as he can at the head or body of the guy with the pads. (It's a motion destined to destroy the rotator cuff of the bowler in a couple of years, but anything for the sport.) The object for the guy with the pads is to keep the thrown ball from knocking down the delicately balanced sticks.

Other guys with zinc oxide all over their noses and lips and big wide white hats stand around in front and in back of the batter and if he hits the ball, even sideways, somebody tries to get it. During this process they get hundreds of runs, and then, after morning tea, a lunch break and afternoon tea, some team wins five days later. It's similar to our baseball games but takes much longer. If one finds it a tad slow, I suppose one could bring a mirror and watch his hair grow.

If my description isn't expurgated, I wish to apologize in advance to my friend, Damon "the Voice" Durant of station FMR in Cape Town, a prominent announcer of cricket matches.

A fierce, sturdy Asian woman, Dr. Frene (pronounced Fay) Gingwala, who in the 1960s published two newspapers and trained a number of journalists, is now speaker of the South African Parliament. Under the new Constitution, committees will have real power, but costly basic management changes need to be made, including the hiring of more clerks and translators. She is determined to make the institution of Parliament more efficient and to make sure that the millions of people who need to be educated about how Parliament actually works are educated. In the old days, the gallery of visitors was just cleared out when there was dissension—and sometimes for no apparent reason.

Madam Speaker initiated the removal of pictures of white history that hung in the Parliament buildings, a new cause for alarm among many white South Africans. The removal of some sculptures and huge oil paintings of parliamentarians, historic events and prominent people—all white—from the beautiful marble halls of the Parliament buildings in Cape Town caused much controversy and while it is not hard to see why the representations are irritating to a large class of people who suffered under apartheid, the symbols are, in fact, part of history. And they are art, albeit some of it bad. Destroying art or books in an effort to change or deny history doesn't work in the long run, but the plan was not to destroy them, just to replace them.

I kept seeing parallels with things in my own country's history. For example, the "stars and bars," the official flag of the Confederacy before and during our own Civil War, is an attractive and historic emblem. While a continuing source of pride for some, it raises hackles for others. We have an organization called the Southern League, which could be the prototype for some organizations in South Africa. They are furious at the dislocation of symbols such as the Confederate flag and the removal of some statues of Confederate fighters to lesser places—and outraged that a likeness of tennis great Arthur Ashe (a black man) would be placed near Confederate heroes (who fought to preserve slavery.)

The League professes to be against slavery, but they sure liked things the way they were in the old days, and some members even claim that the South will rise again when the United States falls of its own weight.

Regional and historic pride is prevalent in the U.S., but while honoring our differences, there is a greater need to recognize our common interests. In my view, the Confederate symbols should not be destroyed or diminished in their historical perspective, but the Confederate flag should not be flown over a state house in the U.S. any more than the old flag of South Africa should be in a superior position to or substituted for the new flag. Too much symbolism of too much pain.

An amazing work of art is the flag of old South Africa made entirely of ostrich feathers in the Ostrich Cooperative in Oudtshoorn. It has been "put away" for now, but soon, I hope, will be on display in a museum.

The paintings from the Parliament building were temporarily replaced with a very disturbing traveling exhibit, "The Art of Apartheid."

A famous trenchant and, to most people, hilariously funny comedian, Pieter Dirk-Uys, has been at work in wigs, lipstick and the latest dowager fashions since well before the birth of the new South Africa. He does one-man shows, plays to packed audiences at clubs and parties and is frequently interviewed on radio and TV as the self-proclaimed "South African ambassador without portfolio." It is hard to see what has kept him out of prison for his irreverent wit—he will skewer the government (any government), any personality, any race, color, creed or situation.

His solution for the statuary dislodged from Parliament is to put each statue in a separate cell on Robben Island, make it a park and charge admission. Robben Island, an essentially inescapable prison several miles off the Cape Town coast (like San Francisco's Alcatraz,) is where President Mandela was imprisoned for about twenty-six years.

Dirk-Uys also does a famous piece called "One vote, one volt."

In southern Africa the matters of land ownership and rights of "traditional peoples" are real headaches and the basis of severe disagreement, sometimes bloodshed, as has been the case in the U.S. Matters are complicated by increasing populations, nastier weapons and many, many borders. Other flies in the ointment are tribal jealousies and the ghastly injustice of land simply being appropriated by various white-dominated governments over the last couple of centuries, to say nothing of servitude, torture and injustice of unparalleled magnitude. Resolving land issues has been likened to trying to unscramble an egg. One of several creative suggestions is "make a cake."

Where I live much of the time, about forty miles north of Mexico, we have many of the border-related problems—hundreds of miles of an invisible line that is continually criss-crossed in many ways—in both directions, legally and illegally.

For example, for a long time the Tohono O'Odham, a large Native American tribe, had learned to adapt to life in the harsh Sonoran Desert. The people lived on long-held lands, which now are divided by the international border. Three million acres and 12,000 people found themselves north of the border, not really integrated or respected by the other Americans, who now live near the reservation boundary. But at least the boundaries and some of the rights of the reservation are acknowledged.

There is no Indian reservation on the Mexican side so, with essentially no protection, a few thousand people of the same tribe live on ancestral lands, which are frequently violated, with no real recourse to defend their land.

Non-native grasses are planted for forage and quick profit by cattle ranchers. Rapidly and irreversibly these grasses crowd out native species, which have been vital to the lives of the indigenous people. Water, an eternal problem, is siphoned off from above and below ground, and mining companies dump their poisonous chemicals almost at will, quickly polluting precious aquifers.

Indigenous peoples have historically been disliked, misunderstood and certainly not honored by their governments in the Americas. Their lot in life has changed in ways beyond their control. Lands that were once Mexican became American. The Gadsden Purchase made much of southern Arizona, including Tucson, part of the United States instead of Mexico. In much of New Mexico Chicanos didn't cross the border, the border crossed them. In wars, grants, annexations and purchases it's not just land that changes hands. People's governments often change, often with disastrous consequences.

Similar boundary changes, actions upon land and water and racial issues complicate the situation in South Africa. The nine provinces (equivalent to our states) have been redrawn and renamed. The Western Cape was renamed the Province of the Cape of Good Hope. The Orange Free State is now just the Free State and Johannesburg is in Gautang, more or less pronounced "how-gurgle gurgle-tang."

Political and economic problems are further compounded by the presence of "internal" tiny, completely autonomous nations. Lesotho is landlocked within South Africa, and Swaziland is surrounded by South Africa with a small segment of common border with Tanzania, but ethnicities and languages cross the invisible borders.

Drugs are beginning to hit the white South African middle class in a big way. Marijuana (dagga), speed (mandrax), cocaine and others have always been there, but now there are younger people with more money and the attitudes that caused—are causing—similar disasters in the States. Not long after I left, an e-mail from a friend who is the equivalent of Cape Town's medical examiner read:

> Our police at mortuary on slow strike because their mortuary allowance was taken away. Last night a big drug lord, Muslim, was executed by being shot, then set alight and finally shot again.

The next few day things escalated dramatically, and Cape Town was terrified of open gang warfare. Out of a population of forty-four million South Africans, about one million were Muslims, very religious, hard working, very family conscious; but as in almost any barrel there was a bad apple. Rashaad Staggie was dealing cocaine and mandrax big-time and was killed as described above.

The community formed People Against Gangsterism and Drugs, PAGAD, a strong, armed vigilante band of about a thousand Muslims in Cape Town, which set out to destroy drugs and gang activity on the theory that the police weren't doing anything. The "warfare" took place mainly in the townships and resulted in a couple of deaths, including the death of a king-pin of a gang called the HLK (Hard Living Kids.) Things finally settled down as the government took swift and severe action, but drugs remain insidious in any culture.

Not many years ago, a black, articulate British-educated Anglican minister, Desmond Tutu, beat on the doors of St. George's Anglican Cathedral in Cape Town to demand admittance for everyone. Just before leaving Cape Town I went to hear Tutu, now archbishop, preach at St. George's, the very church that had denied him admittance for so many years. Once again I observed that humor often can convey a deadly serious matter more effectively than sermonizing. Tutu is a very witty man.

Much of the future, as I see it, depends on the successes of the Truth and Reconciliation Commission during its two year life-span, ending in 1998. The seventeen people, headed by

Archbishop Tutu, are adopting a controversial path, but probably the only one that will work: to grant amnesty to those who step forward and fully confess their crimes, no matter how heinous. The commission is determined to expose to public scrutiny the terrible brutalities of the apartheid years, both by the government and the resistance, black and white, on the theory that, if left undiscussed, old hatreds and injustices will simply fester and eventually poison the whole society. The Mandela policy is that reconciliation is the only way to heal and is essential for survival of the country.

Those who don't come forward are subject to eventual prosecution and perhaps worse, private vengeance. As of this writing, there have already been over 2,000 applications for amnesty, but much weirdness is yet to surface. Recently the remains of a very high-up general in the apartheid regime were found hanging from a tree just below a cliff on the edge of the Indian Ocean. They had become mummified. It wasn't clear whether he had been murdered or committed suicide.

Atrocities have been perpetrated by all races in South Africa over many years. Dealing with the approach of reconciliation and varying views of justice is the job of the commission. It's life of two years seems short to resolve seemingly unresolvable problems.

I was fortunate to have an interesting talk with Bishop Tutu. I gave him several postcards of the beautiful and influential St. Philips in the Hills Episcopal Church in Tucson, with the hope that he would visit there. He was about to retire and had accepted a position at Emory University in Atlanta, Georgia. But, thank God, he was available and was asked to chair the Truth and Reconciliation Commission. To my amazement, when I returned after traveling several months in Namibia and elsewhere, I received a handwritten note from Tutu thanking me for the cards and expressing his desire to visit Tucson. It had been sent to Arizona and forwarded back to me in Cape Town.

In the new South Africa, revenge for injustices done by whites has been wrought upon many innocent white people by black people blinded by rage, indignation or self-righteousness. The recent savage murders of white farmers, especially the wives of white farmers, is constantly on the minds of many present-day farmers.

Ghastly black-on-black violence is everywhere. Who can ever forget the few pictures that made it out of Soweto of black people, men or women, accused of being a traitor by someone, hands tied together with wire as gasoline-soaked rubber tires were put over their heads and lighted—"necklacing"? It turns out that the South African Defense Forces also became experts at provoking necklacing so as to "keep the pot boiling."

White people have been truly cruel to each other in South African history, including now. The Anglo-Boer wars stand out in most people's minds, when the British burned the houses and fields, killed livestock and brutally imprisoned, starved and abused the women and children of non-British white people. Scorched earth and concentration camps weren't invented in World War II.

A characteristic that defined Americans a while back was that almost everyone was closely related to a farmer. Very few white people in South Africa are more than one generation away from being part of a farm, a reality that keeps people in touch with the land, nature and agriculture. Namibia, also, is tied to ranching and farming and intimately linked to South Africa at many levels. Because Namibia is the size of France, with less than 1.5 million people, mostly blacks belonging to distinctly different tribes, it has a different, although overlapping, history.

What kept astonishing me all over southern Africa was how much acceptance and actual love can be found in the most unlikely places. Tolerance, as a strategy for mutual survival, was gradually seeping in. It did not involve forgetting the past and did not necessarily include "forgiving." But awareness was growing that we are all in this together and that there is just so much water, a finite amount of arable land, uneven distributions of mineral resources, and a diminishing willingness to see one's loved ones slaughtered.

Systems are not as they used to be for many reasons, including the sheer number of people participating in the pie. Cooperation is gradually becoming recognized as a necessity—except among "true believers" in one party, religion or cause, who view life differently. I sometimes fantasize about sticking all those people who love war, torture and killing in some remote place and letting them have at it with each other.

While I had little trouble with blacks, whites or others, occasionally I would get a little twinge of feeling about being a distinct numerical subordinate. It was sometimes not a comfortable situation, but it was a useful experience to partially understand how a minority person might feel, especially if it went a few steps further into the repression or deprivation of my rights as I had come to understand them. Personally I believe that all children—all people—should be born into situations where they are wanted and can be provided for, and that all human beings have a right to clean air, clean water, enough to eat, shelter, enough clothes and work that is meaningful.

A vital concept and reality for Americans to keep in mind when trying to comprehend southern Africa is that white people are less than ten percent, not the ninety percent white or latino that we have. There are five million whites, forty-four million people of various colors in South Africa. And I think a necessity for South Africans is to understand what a wonderful, interesting and truly unique national identity it has—a distinctive, multi-faceted South African culture.

In all parts of the world people seem to be tiring of war, separateness and loathing and are beginning to recognize our common interests as humans. A hated enemy soldier blown to bits or hopelessly maimed by the still-abundant anti-personnel land mines all over the world is no more dead or wounded than a farmer who simply hits one while plowing his field. Remnants of the old South Africa still wreak havoc on the new South Africa.

CHAPTER 4

MURDER IN THE GARDEN

Twenty-four hours ago, at eleven in the morning, Mrs. Willard, a seventy-three-year-old somewhat frail white woman, lived alone in her house in Pinelands. Soon Mrs. Willard would be murdered by strangulation with a rag that had one single-turn knot.

From week twenty-one, Cape Town

Gradually people around the world seem to be realizing that violence is never a permanent solution to a problem, even when someone is killed. The gruesome murder and burning of an alleged Muslim drug lord activated a "ready-to-go" group of Muslim vigilantes, PAGAD, mentioned earlier, and simply escalated the violence. It didn't solve anything in the larger sense. Fundamentalist approaches seem to be getting mixed in with legal and law enforcement issues, and gang violence seems to have gone too far to be stopped by conventional methods. I guess it's one of those things that must just play itself out. Ugly.

But it still amazes me how, after all the murderous events on all sides during the apartheid years, the government of South Africa can have a policy of reconciliation rather than of vengeance. It is incredibly civilized, in my view, when a characteristic of our world still seems to be murder everywhere. I am not qualified to make statistical comparisons, but my observation was that there were fewer guns in the hands of average people in southern Africa than in the States. So murders often take more physical forms.

My first morning in Cape Town I was seated on the patio of a restaurant in Tamboeskloff. A sunny, lovely spring morning.

At the next table two men were having breakfast, and one told a joke, which I couldn't help overhearing. I laughed. Cautiously they looked over at me then invited me to come sit with them. Both were doctors.

Dr. Gideon Jacobus Knobel, head of forensic medicine in the University of Cape Town medical school, was having breakfast with an old friend. We talked about recent autopsies that Knobel had conducted and a complicated operation that his friend, an anesthesiologist, had just come from.

We became friends, and when I returned from several months traveling the country, we re-established contact and I told Knobel about my car accident. He had just come from the mortuary and glibly commented that I was lucky I hadn't ended up on one of those marble slabs. I had never thought about it that way, and it hit me like a ton of bricks that I could have been killed. Dead.

I began to think about all those lives suddenly ended, often in grisly fashion. What would have happened had I been killed? Who would ever have known (or cared) what was in my computer or who were the intended recipients of the trinkets I had acquired? How long would I have been lying there? And then what? What is the life strand, so easily broken? The thought kept turning over in my head—and still does.

Dr. Knobel made several rare opportunities possible for me, such as attendance at the International Conference of Forensic Pathologists and medical trips to some of the poorest townships. One day he invited me to attend his lecture on grieving, followed by autopsies, which is a requirement for fourth-year medical students.

As a nonfiction writer I had written a number of medical stories over the years, some on death and dying, but somehow the possibility of attending an autopsy and what I might learn had never occurred to me. Expanding my understanding of life and death became a large factor in my decision. Inexorable inquisitiveness is a necessary trait of a nonfiction writer, and this was a rare opportunity, which many, even the curious few, would immediately decline. Even the intrepid would mull, especially after the recently concluded O.J. Simpson trial, which was widely covered in South Africa.

I have a very low threshold for blatant horror, so I thought for a long while and then asked such questions as:

"Is it bloody?"

"Some," was his response.

"Does it smell bad?"

"Sometimes. Depends on the case. We don't know just what will show up each day."

These autopsies were conducted to determine causes of death, and the results were often used in court cases. A police photographer is present to constantly take flash pictures of each stage and discovery.

"Do you think I could handle it?"

"One never knows," he replied. "The most unexpected people faint."

"Can I leave in the middle?"

"Yes."

After a number of other questions I tentatively accepted the offer. We had done a number of things together and seemed to understand each other quite well. I was, and remain, struck by his humor, and above all by his understanding, compassion and courtesy. It was agreed that I attend the lecture and then would make up my mind if I wanted to proceed.

While I have a high tolerance for stressful situations, I wondered whether I was prepared to actually see what I thought he was saying I would see. Curiosity, not really morbid curiosity but profound, respectful curiosity, led me toward looking at the dead…those whose lives were snuffed and just the bony, fleshy residue of a person is left to view. Millions more people struggle on for a while and the billions that have already lived have evaporated.

How would I handle someone whose brain has been cracked out of it's shell while my skull is just dented? What is a life? What about torture victims? What were these kinds of death really like?

At the public mortuary in Cape Town, in a lecture hall, a dozen bright, young fourth-year medical students, male and female, one white, one Indian and the rest black or brown, were indistinguishable from any other students in dress, hair styles and general appearance. They hailed from several countries in southern Africa, and even the untrained ear could hear that several languages were being spoken as we waited to begin. During the "introduce yourself" period, one large, rather stern-looking young black woman said she was from Mozambique. With a smile Dr. Knobel instantly said some things to her in her own tongue which caused her to change completely into a smiling, responsive person. These kids would soon go back to their homes and become *the* medical personnel. Knobel's preoccupation was with their becoming competent and, above all, compassionate doctors.

The lecture was a delicate handling of death, dying and the grieving process. Several people, including me, were called upon to say something about the death of a loved one. Some of the stories were highly emotional—a parent with a limb blown off died in one student's arms. A young man whose sister had disappeared wondered, almost weeping, if she was on a slab in some mortuary in a neighboring country. The whole thing was wrenching, but handled with grace and delicacy in such a way that the group, including me, felt very bound together in our humanity and sadness. "Remember," Knobel said, "behind every dead body is a grieving family."

I decided to go for it. We donned white plastic aprons and blue paper shoe covers, were given face masks with elastic that fit over each ear and filed into the mortuary. Knobel and several workers were there in big plastic aprons, rubber gloves and tall rubber boots. Knobel's boots had his name written along the top.

I was one of the first in the room and stood by the side of the table upon which a double thickness of sheet covered a small form. The green cloth was clean and pressed but a little frayed on one edge. How many bodies had this covered? They did about 3,500 of these autopsies a year, sometimes thirty in one day.

Knobel gently lifted back the cloth, uncovering a little black girl, perhaps two years old, who had died of dehydration and maybe other deficiencies. But she had suffered no physical or sexual abuse, he explained as he talked about both—a matter of factual necessity. He explained why the freshly dead body was no longer stiff, and to my relief closed the baby's dark eyes. We looked at a lot, but there was no need to cut. He gently pinched the skin in several places. It stood up in little pyramids, a sure sign of dehydration, he explained. He then gently rubbed the deformities away.

There were three other tables, three bodies discreetly covered, dead less than twenty hours. He gently but firmly reminded the students that someone was grieving over each of these dead people. As we assembled around another table, a fifth body was wheeled in, a man killed in a suspicious and grisly auto accident. Knobel gently lifted back the cloth just far enough to expose the legs of a white person. Pink flesh oozed slightly where strips of skin had been removed. Knobel explained that the family had generously donated skin for a number of children that had been burned in a township fire the day before. It made me think of a friend's parents who had been hideously burned over eighty percent of their bodies and the pain, horror and ugliness of their grafts. But without the grafts they would have died.

Then came Mrs. Willard. We looked at the body for a long time, examining bruises, the knot in the strangulation cloth, the colors and marks on her body. I kept looking at the tan shipping tag with a big black number written on it tied to her left big toe with white string. The baby had one too.

An assistant handed Knobel a sealed white styrofoam box. He wrote the toe-tag number on the front, broke the seal, and inside, bottles, envelopes and paraphernalia for collecting samples were in sealed bags. After collections the box would be re-sealed and signed by him and sent to the crime laboratory in Johannesburg.

A clump of hair was plucked from her still-bloody head with tweezers and put in an envelope. Some hairs were tweezed from the pubis, and a pink comb was raked gently over the pubis in case there were any other hairs. The comb and the samples were put in another envelope. An inch-long cut was made in the left groin. Blood began to flow out. He collected several small bottles for typing and other tests. With long Q-tips he took samples from the vagina and nose, made smears on glass slides and put each swab and slide in a separate envelope. An assistant immediately put the evidence in the styrofoam box.

What did I think? Hard for me to say. I looked at this naked woman, her eyes opened to show blood spots and capillary damage, the strangulation cloth cut off and put in the styrofoam box as the police photographer kept snapping flash pictures. What was I thinking about Mrs. Willard's life and mine? She was seven years older than I was. Yesterday she was alive, working in her garden. I looked into her pale blue eyes, but she was looking somewhere else. I felt very, very sad.

Knobel announced that the next step was to open the skull, a procedure, he said, that bothers many people because of the noise of the saw. He suggested that anyone who wanted to take a break could, but to be back in ten minutes. Most left. The girl from Mozambique and I went over and stood by the door. I didn't know about her, but I wanted to be able to leave quickly if I needed to.

The attendant took a scalpel, made some long cuts along the back and sides of the scalp and then yanked the scalp up and forward so the flap lay down over her forehead. It was a ripping sound that I will never forget. I thought of stories about our Indians and others scalping and being scalped. I closed my eyes for a minute and took a deep breath. There was a large dark red spot on her skull—the bruise from a blow.

A specialized saw cut around the white skull with what was indeed an unpleasant sound. The attendant then picked up a silver object about the size of a candy bar but with one long edge tapered. He wedged it into the saw cut and rocked it a couple of times. I heard a cracking sound like opening a coconut—again a sound that I will not forget.

The top of the skull was lifted off gently, exposing the brain in its thin, transparent bag. Again there was a dark patch indicating that the blow to the head had caused bleeding under the skull. From where I stood I could see that Mrs. Willard's eyes were shielded by the flap of skin of her own scalp.

To make more viewing room for the students who were now filing back, two men swung her around on the smooth stainless steel table so that her head was now up near the other end, and with huge white sponges wiped the table clean. The table, which had only this one purpose, was crimped on the diagonals so the drainage was to the center. A vertical pipe drained directly down from the center into a grillwork hole in the floor.

The brain was eased out, everything was examined and pointed out. As we looked down into the floor of the empty skull, Knobel stripped away more and more tissues, massaging blood out so that this was what he called "a bloodless autopsy." At every stage the assistants tried to keep the table and body free of excess blood. I was a bit taken aback as dark red bubbles began to seep from her mouth. But Knobel was so gentle and explained it so well that one felt his respect for the body.

Knobel made one long, deft, swift cut from the throat to the pubis and talked as he opened the body cavity and laid back the flaps of the skin. Each flap was completely lined with a thick, grainy, bright yellow layer of fat globules. He examined everything for irregularities that might have contributed to or even been the cause of death. This was all for court—hopefully a murder trial soon. He felt confident, without explaining why or how, that the killer would be caught soon.

How much strength had the killer used in a knife murder? This was a question always asked at trials. Delicately Knobel took a knife like a kitchen boning knife and made one stab at her below her left breast. Very little, practically no force, like stabbing into a rotten log. Then he took the knife and stabbed again right over a rib. Much more force was needed to penetrate, but Knobel explained that already her bones are thinning from age.

A breast still attached to the huge flap of skin lay meaninglessly on the table. I was struck by the colors of the inside of the body—the yellow fat, the blues, the pinks, the reds and grays and whites. And the shapes—most identifiable, especially the intestines.

The breast bone was cutaway with a heavy black-handled knife by a strong assistant and lifted out as one might do when boning a chicken. Knobel and an assistant gently ladled the intestine, the lungs, liver, pancreas and other stuff with strong gloved hands and put them into large red plastic buckets. Knobel explained as each organ was removed what signs to look for in determining the actual cause of death. A knot was tied in the end of the small intestine to hold in the contents of the stomach, critical evidence in some cases.

Surprisingly few tools were used in this whole process. The fat-covered heart was removed and cut in two to show what he said was a strong heart in amazingly good condition. Various veins and arteries were cut open and revealed no clogging. He was very impressed. The lungs showed some collapse (the dark blue) and some emphysema (the lighter, dull pink), all of which was explained.

What really got to me was when Knobel cut the ribs apart from each other and pressed on the ends to see if any were fractured. None were, but they stood up like a bleached carcass in the desert. I looked away, but for better or worse I will always see that picture in my mind.

He slit the trachea. It looked like it was made of clear white plastic, and sounded like it was plastic. As he laid it open, one could see the bifurcating carotid artery. Again he was impressed at what a wonderful example it was, and handed it to an assistant to be taken back to the medical museum in a little bucket of fluid.

We left this ungainly mess, the half head, the face partially pulled back up, the individual ribs sticking up above the rest, blood carefully mopped up, and moved back to the baby's table. The limp little thing had one small pyramid of skin still sticking up below its left nipple. Knobel stroked it down as one might pick off a piece of lint and gently pushed the baby up to the head of its table, like a doll, to make room for the several buckets of Mrs. Willard's organs.

What was I thinking about life, and life and death and about various kinds of death? The baby, the man in the accident, Mrs. Willard. Mrs. Willard was a real person to me. So what of the soul or whatever is the part of a life that is no more? My meditation was interrupted as Knobel cut a kidney in two. No damage, he said and sometimes there was in these violent situations. He made three slices into the liver. Other parts were individually examined; the pancreas, the vagina, the ovaries and uterus, the rectum. Something had a matte finish, rather than a smooth surface, indicating her age and loss of estrogen. I couldn't tell by looking at it what it was and didn't want to interrupt.

I glanced back at Mrs. Willard's table. The arm of a large black man in boots and a white apron slowly rose up as though he were pulling a long sewing thread. That's exactly what he was doing. The lower part of her belly was held together by four or five large X's, stitches perhaps two inches long, each made with a coarse brown thread.

The man looked up with an expressionless face as a student asked Knobel what was to become of "these materials," meaning the stuff in the red buckets. Knobel pointed over at the man who was sewing and said that the organs would be returned to the body cavity. Then the opening would be closed and Mrs. Willard would be returned to her family for burial.

Who had killed her? Could it have been the guy on the next table with the bullet entry wound near the lower right jaw and an exit wound through the top of his head? Typical gang execution. He lay on the table just a few feet from her. We walked over to examine him, his gang tattoos, his limp penis and large tight testicles, his pale skin and expressionless face. I was grateful that his eyes were closed. I was standing at the foot of the table. On his right shin from knee to ankle it said MONEY, and on the left one it said LOVER in large blue capital letters. The letters took on a greenish hue because of the sallowness of his skin. The coloured gang member—family? Missed for a minute by a few, I hope. So life is death, and there's always a tomorrow with new bodies on the tables.

By that point we had been in the room two hours. Not much had been said about the circumstances surrounding the charred body of a black man on another table. We circled around him but stood still and respectful. I thought of the butterflies in Oudtshoorn.

It must be the convention to lay the penis up and to the right. Crispy blacker-than-black pieces of skin were about to fall off the body like old paint. Had a survivor of the flames that killed him received some of the layers of skin from the first man we saw?

Would the baby have been better off not to have been born? Would Mrs. Willard have fallen and broken her hip in a few years? Perhaps. But surely her terror could not have been as great as when someone tied the knot in the rag around her throat. I hoped she had been unconscious from the blow.

Mrs. Willard was what Knobel called a "soft target," an

elderly person living alone in her house in a pleasant suburb of Cape Town, Pinelands. Who had done it? Why?

I myself would want to be totally consumed, down to ashes.

CHAPTER 5

OLD SOUTH AFRICA, OLD AMERICA

The news…set up a great disturbance of submarine currents and cross-currents in the black deeps…of which the foam of white people, floating gently on the surface, were entirely unaware.

In Face of Fear *by Freda Troup*

The auto accident had changed my body, my life, my wallet and my plans, but I was ready to move on from a fascinating month in Pretoria. My friends, the Tom de Villiers in Arizona, former ostrich farmers from near Oudtshoorn, had referred me to their good friends, also named de Villiers, who lived near Beaufort West in the Great Karoo. (Being a de Villiers in South Africa is like being a Smith in the States.) The Murray de Villiers family were the fourth generation owners of a sheep farm called La De Da, a name which I doubt would seriously be bestowed in this more callous day and age. I had been told that it was one of the oldest and most beautiful farms in the Karoo and that they had a guest house that they "let out" (rented). Perfect.

Phone contact was not always the easiest in South Africa and became even more iffy when one was calling a farm. Party lines and technical problems still abounded. Finally we made a connection, and with total cordiality Murray de Villiers said to come ahead. Things had changed quite a bit, he said, but they would be glad to put me up. He said something about the farm being in the process of being sold and that they had to take the kids back to boarding school next week but that I was welcome to stay as long as I cared to.

I questioned, but he assured me and said he would meet my bus at 6:30 Friday morning, one of the several times a week the bus passed through Beaufort West, the self-designated "Capital of the Great Karoo." After the all-night trip from Pretoria, the bus stopped briefly in the center of town, then hurried on its still lengthy trip to Cape Town.

Murray, a ruggedly handsome young man with blood-shot eyes, grabbed my luggage from the curb, put it carefully in the back of the pickup truck (called a bakkie). He introduced himself as Murray, gave me an unexpected kiss on the lips (a common practice in South Africa, but startling for Americans at first) and asked if I had had breakfast. No, so we drove to the Sunshine Cafe. Bacon and fried eggs for him—cholesterol apprehension apparently hadn't really hit the Karoo yet, or at least not this man. He bowed his head and then, looking up with his hands still folded, asked me if I said grace.

I bowed my head, having learned that grace was a very widely practiced custom. After a long heartfelt blessing, which included thanks that I had arrived safely, he started to eat and promptly began an oration on the evils of liberation theology and what an evil man Desmond Tutu was. Adam and Eve was a bit much for me at seven in the morning after an all-night bus trip, so while acknowledging that his religion clearly was important to him, I laboriously shifted the conversation to the farm.

We then drove around town, which was very still. "My great-grandfather built that Methodist church" he said pointing as we slowly drove by. "There's the Chris Barnard home and museum." Yes, I assured him, I knew that Dr. Barnard had performed the first heart transplant. "My great-grandfather built that dam," he said as we drove by a huge grassy berm. "And that's Matoppo House, which Grandfather inherited along with La De Da when his second wife died."

We drove further to the outskirts, a modest but not clearly slummy section on the south side where the black people lived. He needed to talk to a girl about coming out to do some work next week. He said that they had had to let most of the help go, but this girl was very good, and he thought she would work out if they could get her properly trained.

And so it went. Very interesting to me, but it turned out that we were also passing time until the small supermarket opened. He needed to buy some things for his wife.

We drove south past the entrance to the Karoo National Park on the N-1 highway to Cape Town and further into a seemingly endless basin flanked by bare flat-top mountains with desert-like scrub. The terrain resembled parts of Arizona. I felt right at home. We turned and drove a couple of miles on a dirt road and then turned again at some attractive, professionally painted signs under a neat banner saying M.L de Villiers, the only evidence of mankind in sight except for some fence. One sign said Merino Stud with a picture of a very wooly Merino sheep. The other had a picture of a black-face Dorper sheep and said Dorper Stud. He explained that because of the drought the land wouldn't handle very many sheep, even though he was luckier than many because his land had a number of good springs, which he called fountains. It was hard enough to keep even the best breeding stock fit during the drought, he explained.

There was nothing but open rolling land as we drove several miles further. I spotted the tips of cypress trees, and then as we drove down and over a dry wash and up the other bank—an oasis. A big old green wagon at the fenced entrance had a discreet sign emblazoned La De Da.

We drove down a straight road flanked by giant old jacaranda trees that his mother had planted forty years ago. The purple blossoms were past their peak but still beautiful. He pointed at an empty field. "I had to tear out a couple of acres of oranges because there wasn't enough water. The new owner is thinking about putting in olives or maybe grapes. If he starts making wine, I'll have to leave. Even though wine is in the Bible, I've seen it cause too much trouble and sin."

Orchards on the right, and manicured lawns, tree roses, lovely plantings and a huge old white house with a traditional thatched roof on the left. It was all breathtaking.

At the end of the road was a smaller building with covered parking for a tractor and other vehicles. A very attractive young woman, Murray's wife, Mariette, stood with four beautiful, healthy children ranging from eight to fifteen, waiting to greet us. "Say hello to Auntie Martha," she said. Simultaneously they said "Hello, Auntie Martha," but the twinkle was there and I knew instantly that I liked them. Auntie was the customary, courteous way that an "elderly person" was greeted. I didn't feel elderly, but there it was. Some of my grandchildren were older than the youngest of these kids.

Understanding the "new South Africa" requires some understanding of the "old South Africa"...both periods rich in history and complexities. Some of the awareness that grew in me was based on a partial understanding of my own past and of the history of my own country. But apparently the mirror of old South Africa was required for me to see more clearly.

I was to stay in the now-vacant old mansion and, for a while, to share the lives of the last generation of de Villiers to own this lovely place. Not only was the big house intact, but the huge trees, the irrigation systems, the rose gardens, vineyards and orchards near the house were thriving. The ancient dry-laid stone kraal (corral), the windmills, roads, miles of grazing land, workers' cottages, a swimming pool blasted out of bedrock and all the elements of what we would probably call a plantation were there.

This year had to be one of the worst times in the lives of Murray and Mariette—they had moved out of the big house a few weeks ago and into the little cottage they used to let out (the one that I had anticipated renting) to deal with little help, inadequate kitchen facilities, uncertainties about money and oh-so-many other problems in the middle of an increasingly hot Karoo summer. There were few complaints, even from the children.

As soon as the documents of sale had been completed, as a point of honor (their honor) the family moved out of the big house so that it could be cleaned and brought up to snuff for the new owner. The new owners' plans were to develop a guest farm, put in some olive orchards and maybe run some ostrich. Proper living quarters would be created for the de Villiers family and the family would stay on in complete charge, with Murray doing the sheep and everything more or less as it always had been done. The feelings about the future were good, but the money wouldn't change hands for a few more days.

I had no idea of all these problems, or I never would have come to visit them. And if I had been Mariette, I probably would have said no to a visitor. Yet unbounded hospitality seemed to be a near-universal trait of South Africans.

But there I was, still somewhat shaken by my auto accident; and transportation out of Beaufort West would perhaps pose more of a problem than I had getting there from Pretoria. So I decided to stay on and be as painless a guest as possible. A bed and a few necessities had been put back in one of the many bedrooms in the big house for me. The next ten days were among the most pleasant and interesting of my life.

The Henry Ford mansion, Fair Lane, in Dearborn, Michigan probably wouldn't be called a plantation, but there were many similarities to La De Da that gradually and unexpectedly caused many memories of my childhood to flood back.

A circumstance that has been troublesome to me throughout my life is the fact that Henry Ford was, by marriage, my father's uncle. Henry married another simple Detroiter, Clara Bryant. To many that was wonderful; but the result was not without its problems for the concentric rings of relatives, especially when the Fords became some of the world's wealthiest and most famous people.

My father publicly, and I think privately, worshipped Henry Ford, and to some, including me, was boringly devout whenever that subject came up. And Uncle Henry came up a lot.

My mother, on the other hand, was increasingly contemptuous of the Fords (and eventually of my father). But in hindsight I believe her to have been correct that my father's relationship with Henry Ford denied much to my dad. He rarely could do anything creative without someone attributing it to the Ford connection. And people always assumed that we had money because of the relationship.

My father earned a good living at the peak of the Roaring Twenties, as a smart young lawyer with a witty, beautiful but often acerbic young lawyer wife. There were perks from the relationship with the Fords, like freighter trips on the Great Lakes on the large fleet of ships carrying iron ore from Lake Superior mines to the Rouge Plant on the Detroit River, and parties and other functions at mansions and other locales. But to my knowledge, my father never received penny one from the Fords, and I think he never expected to. All this was before the Great Depression (which badly damaged my family) and before my conscious time. (I was born in the April before the great crash in October of 1929.)

I really didn't know "Uncle Henry" but I have specific recollections of corpulent, abrupt, opinionated and forceful Aunt Clara at Fair Lane. Not a very pleasant person to this child's eye, but children's views on such matters were generally not solicited and kept private in my family.

I distinctly remember being taken out of school to attend Henry Ford's funeral. It was a cold, wet and dreary day, and everyone looked miserable; so I put on a cold, dreary and miserable expression, which is evident in a picture I recently found. I hated the school I was in, so for me it was a zero-sum day—not the moment of history my father kept telling me it was.

As long as my father lived he insisted on our frequently visiting Greenfield Village, Henry Ford's big-time collection of Americana. Every time we had to visit the Martha-Mary Chapel (names of Henry's and Clara's mothers), which, my Dad maintained I was named after. Both good biblical names.

My mother contended, however, that I was named after Martha Carrier, a direct ancestor on her side, who was hanged as the "Queen of Hell" during the Salem witch trials. Soon after her death, Martha was totally exonerated by the confessions of the hysterical teenage girls who had accused her. I gather that Martha was considered unpleasant because of her outspoken comments about many things, including absurdities in the law. These two divergent origins are perhaps why I didn't like my name when I was young. But I have become very accustomed to it now and frankly prefer the latter version of origin.

As I soaked up the feelings surrounding me at La De Da, I began to reflect on the similar roles Caucasian women of wealth have and their position through history. Repeatedly since arriving in the southern hemisphere I had observed that classes and groups of people were the same as I had observed elsewhere in the world and through the course of history as I understood it. I wondered if someone had yet developed or studied a lateral theory of class.

The woman, who sometimes brought money to the marriage though inheritance, was in charge of the house and the servants but could always be overridden by the master. She sewed, gardened and was involved in the arts and other "lady things." She attended worthy social causes, founded hospitals for poor blind children and during wars "supported the boys" by rolling bandages and knitting socks. Some ladies temporarily turned over a few buildings as rest and recreation sites for returning soldiers. (South Africa always has had strong armies and has participated in many world conflicts.) The madam was in charge of arranging social occasions and was expected to produce and raise fine children—with the aid of an ample staff. She was not conscious overtly, if at all, that the very system in which she prospered sometimes induced or perpetuated the problems and lower classes she professed to help.

In South Africa, the children of the mansion, especially the girls, were sent away to boarding school unless they were close enough to a town to commute or board for the week and attend the public school. In the very upper classes in the U.S., public schools still aren't usually viewed as "good enough" or socially adequate.

South African boys would, it was hoped, master cricket, rugby, riding, social graces and other manly arts, and the eldest male, as principal heir, would be intensely trained in all elements of the management of the property and business. In the hardworking and prosperous class of white farm families, he was expected to know every fence post, blade of grass, rock, rill, plant, sheep and domestic animal and the habits of all of the wild animals. He would be trained in animal husbandry and the feeding and care of the servants. He was a courteous, well-bred gentleman and a dutiful husband and father. In that day and age, girls were trained to be like their mothers.

Black or coloured people in South Africa were carefully trained to be servants, and much of that attitude remained evident.

"Don't speak unless spoken to," stay out of sight and be totally respectful of the dominant person was the system that prevailed in most households, although in others, as on American plantations, a dominant servant often had substantial influence

63

on the "masters." Loyalties between owners and servants could be strong and was evident at La De Da.

A real joy to my very American ear was to hear the impeccable British accent of even the most humble laborer. The servants in almost any household spoke more beautiful English than did most high school seniors I had met in the U.S. Vocabulary might have been a bit short, but diction and clarity were wonderful, perhaps because they had been taught to speak that way since childhood regardless of their ultimate level of schooling.

Liquor was a no-no at La De Da and the Fords, too, were prudish about that and many other things as well. The distaste for and distrust of alcohol was another common thread at both La De Da and Fair Lane, not always the case on large estates in those lush days of entertaining in both countries. (According to my parents, parties thrown by some of the Ford children could be very wet, especially during the days of Prohibition, when many people drank too much.)

Apparently, when there was lots of prosperity at La De Da, friends would come up from Cape Town to visit, but not to party or drink the legendary South African wines. As is often the case anywhere, anytime, the number of one's friends seems to diminish as one's fortunes flag. The Fords' fortunes just seemed to multiply.

At Fair Lane and La De Da, church, religion, God and country were paramount for everyone, regardless of class, although church services were separate for blacks and whites. I began to understand more about my father's extreme racism. It wasn't until he had been around for more than three quarters of a century that he began to change.

At his funeral, his minister told me that the last months of my father's eighty-four-year-long life were spent in fervent prayer, saying "Help me, God. I must learn not to hate black people." All I can say is "Bless you Daddy."

It was difficult to be a boy or a girl who didn't exactly fit the mold in those days. Edsel Ford, according to my Mother (and others), was the most sensitive member of the Ford family and was vigorously berated by his parents, especially his father, Henry.

There is nothing Murray de Villiers didn't know about La

De Da and all it contains, but he said he was mildly dyslexic and berated himself for not having the business sense or political savvy of his forbearers. At least while I was there, he refused to look at the possibility of nine years of drought being a cause of his business failure in a heavily water-dependent business.

As we were driving south from Beaufort West along the N-1 on the day I arrived, the land that we had traversed had a few sprigs of green and so didn't look so utterly desperate. The new growth was due to the first rain in years, which had begun just a few days earlier. Too late. Things had gotten so dire over the years that the plants and animals had died, and the rivers and creeks were dry, as were most springs except, fortunately, those around the house and an occasional small one in a far distant pasture. The land was parched and black and was unable to generate money, Murray said. The property simply had to be sold.

I arrived after the transaction had been completed, and the property's sale was simply a matter of the escrow closing. The large check was supposed to arrive that week. But I began to realize that for the last few weeks it had been touch and go for the family about everything that cost money. A strong sense of pride as well as stubbornness played a role, and I silently agreed with Mariette that Murray was a prime candidate for heart attack. It was the old business of bad things happening to good people, and these were very decent people.

I commented to Murray on how beautiful the gardens looked. Abruptly he said, "You can let everything run down and get dilapidated, and people know this guy's in financial trouble, or go out in a blaze of glory." I looked up at the heavy bunches of plump, ripening grapes hanging from the pergola leading out to the rose garden and said nothing.

We took meals at the little house. I tried to be courteous about retreating to my quarters at appropriate times, which gave me plenty of opportunity to examine and cogitate on the wonderful old structure that Murray's father had built for his mother.

Empty built-in bookcases were in several rooms, including the study where a small desk had been left (or put?). I turned the desk so that my computer cord could reach one of the few plugs. The small fireplace was at my back, and above the rich oiled wainscoting to my right were imposing portraits of the three progenitors, with labels proclaiming "Great Grandfather inherited La De Da [from his second wife who died], Grandfather tamed it, and Father developed it." Sardonically Murray said "And Murray lost it." I know the poor guy felt bad, but the self-flagellation got to me and I said "How about a picture of you saying "…and Murray transitioned La De Da into the twenty-first century?"

He immediately started in (again) saying that the new owners' wishes would prevail. I have learned that, fortunately, the new owner was reputed to be a decent and imaginative person who planned to develop the property as a high-class tourist "guest farm," taking advantage of the proximity to the freeway, the water, the charm and the history. I can think of much worse fates.

As I dutifully did my writing to the hum of the distant generator, which was on for four hours in the early morning and at suppertime, I could gaze through the large sash windows at the spacious, groomed lawn, rose bushes and lovely old trees and plantings. The windows started about eighteen inches above the floor (a single almost knotless plank formed the wide baseboard) and ended at the ornate empty drapery rods. Each window, trimmed in attractive brown wood, had twelve window panes in the top half and twelve in the bottom, and fine brass hardware, all always kept spotless by the servants.

The heavy sash cords reminded me of my childhood home, which my parents had built with bricks from an old bank that was being demolished. I had lived there until I was five years old, and, for unknown reasons, had cut one of the cords—with great difficulty, as I recall—just to see what would happen. I can still hear the loud thud of the heavy, cylindrical lead weight crashing to the bottom of the sash. Expense was beyond my comprehension at that time, but I do remember the workmen laboriously dismantling the window frame to replace the cord and re-hang the counterweight.

There are so many beautiful woods in Africa, many being used up in the same way as tropical forests and redwood forests are being consumed. Redwood is a famous American wood; yellow wood has a similar symbolism in South Africa. I had a flawless, smooth clear-grained lovely little yellow wood table next to my bed in the big house. The dining room chairs were made of stinkwood, a velvety, dense medium-brown wood. Nobody could tell me why it had that name. Subsequently I learned that stinkwood is also much prized for many things, including making the finest xylophones as well as expensive furniture.

Considering the wood floors, wood paneling and thick thatch roof, the large red fire extinguisher that hung by every door in every room seemed like a very good idea. Hanging on a peg outside the French doors leading to the formal rose garden at the end of the house opposite the orchards was a peculiar instrument, a very long thin wooden handle capped with a tilted square board that was randomly pock-marked. Murray explained that it was used occasionally to tamp the butt ends of the foot-thick, sharply trimmed thatch back up. A properly made and cared for thatch roof can last for many decades.

Quickly I fell into the family routines and would appear about half an hour before mealtime to chat and do what I could. But with so many hands and such a small kitchen I usually ended up talking to Murray or one of the kids—just being the honored auntie.

Early every morning I would take a walk in the bright and totally serene picture-perfect countryside, ending up in the orchards, testing out which of the numerous varieties of plums would yield my morning treats. I have lots of Canadian ancestry, and as a child I remember going to visit relatives in the Niagara fruit belt. Perfect peaches hanging at a child's eye level—waiting to be plucked and eaten by me. What a perfect re-living, I thought. I would move to another tree and harvest some warm, perfect specimens to take to the family breakfast and a small bunch of grapes if I could find ripe ones.

Apparently Murray's mother had simply gone through the catalog and ordered one of every fruit tree, and there they were, thriving just outside the back door. The orange trees had been pulled out because of the drought, but almost nothing can stop a mulberry tree—one of God's most delicious and messy fruits.

Again, this took me back to my youth as an incorrigible mulberry eater. I volunteered to pick a bowl for breakfast, a gracefully accepted offer. Mariette, with a puckish smile that she would squelch just enough to let you know that a joke was involved, handed me a huge bowl.

The next day was again a warm beautiful morning. I was out at the mulberry trees about seven and shortly was "covered with blood" as juice flowed from every pick and ran over my hand and down my arm. Big splotches on my face revealed my picking theory—pick two, eat one. When I saw myself in a mirror I was reminded of the auto accident, and suddenly my head felt tender. Cleaning up would be the first time since the crash that I would wash my hair with regular shampoo rather than the medicated stuff the doctor had given me.

Preceded by grace, of course, meals were regular, delicious and, unlike many family gatherings at which I have found myself, pleasant, often fun—and sometimes unnecessarily tense in an interesting way. Straight arrow that he was, Murray was too tough to learn from most people, and sometimes a little hard to deal with if you were a kid. We were talking about range management and invasion by unwanted species. "Kill everything— the plants, the animals, everything—and start over," he said, to the horror of several of the kids. He really did have a sense of preserving and fostering the best a piece of land has to offer, but the way it was put and the lack of an explained, underlying rationale were startling and upsetting to the children.

As a curious and uninvolved third party, I could ask questions that the kids were eager to hear answered. For example, I asked him to explain his "kill everything" statement. A reasoned and artfully put response followed, something to the effect that a hectare of land in this climate could only handle a certain number of sheep and a certain number of big wild game, and they needed certain plants at this season and certain other plants in the winter. The conversations would then open up into discussions.

Lunch was followed by a rest time, universally observed in South Africa, especially now that the days were becoming quite hot. But then, ah-ha—swimming. The pool was a short hike up the hill, beyond the two gigantic mulberry trees and up a steep set of wooden stairs. Murray's grandfather had blasted a great hole in a knob of bedrock and built a good-sized swimming pool, perhaps fifteen meters long, complete with a finished flatrock deck. Grass and trees grew around three sides and the water was always fresh—constantly refreshed by a natural fountain. Mariette and I sat in the shade of several big trees, on an old yellow wagon tailgate that had been converted into a comfortable bench, and brushed away the tiny black and very annoying mosquitoes. We shared the very effective small bottle of 100% DEET insect repellent I had brought along.

We had wonderful talks about everything from WordPerfect computer software, with which she, as an English-speaking person, converted the Afrikaans school lessons into English for her own and other children. We talked of AIDS, kids, life and times, history, such classic world problems as loss and gain.

Her Father, Dr. Theodore "Teti" Germond, had been a missionary in the small independent country of Lesotho, which sits like a sky island, completely surrounded by South Africa, near the east-central coast. Recognizing that the body must be in reasonable order to accept spiritual guidance, Teti studied medicine, became a doctor and returned to Lesotho. He was a very consistent man. For example, the story was often told about how a drunk black fellow with no driver's license crashed a stolen car into Dr. Germond. After recovering from his own severe injuries, the good doctor visited the driver in jail and did many things to help the fellow and his family.

Mariette and her two siblings were highly educated in South Africa but then traveled and worked in Europe before returning to South Africa.

As black nationalism grew throughout Africa, although he was much loved and honored, Dr. Germond was for all practical purposes forced out of practice by black nationalists in Lesotho who made death threats hoping that if the doctor left the other white people would leave. Realizing also that if he died his wife and family would have few possessions and economic security, he left.

As the children's Christmas vacation was about to end and the "day of the check" approached, Murray was around more often and seemed more relaxed. Soon the girls would head back to boarding school near Cape Town, and the young boys would go to the local school in town; but still it was swimming time, and Murray and Mariette were as rowdy as the kids.

In the late afternoon or evening the kids would be on bellies and elbows on the floor making Monopoly deals, but later everything would be picked up and tidy in the very small living room. To me there was no visible sense of resentment that the two girls shared a small single bedroom or that the two boys shared one smaller than the smallest room in the big house.

One afternoon we went far out into the countryside (still on the farm) with rubber rafts and swimsuits to picnic by a dam that Murray's grandfather had built. For the first time I heard mention of a bit of past dissension in Murray's family. Apparently one uncle had sold off his inheritance without even telling Murray, who would have bought it and thereby extended La De Da to the crest of a distant mountain ridge. It turns out that the land was soon to be added to the Karoo National Park; but Murray's hurt was still apparent.

Another evening we played cricket and we all agreed that I was hopeless—you are *not* supposed to drop the bat, which I promptly did as any self-respecting softball player would. Several nights we had a braai (barbecue) outdoors under the old jacarandas, with the traditional coiled string of farmer's sausage and an infinite number of the most delicious lamb and pork chops I have ever had. All raised and slaughtered on the farm.

The children remained impeccably courteous, but over the course of time true enthusiasm began to burst out and I began to sense a private rapport with each of them. It was special for me to have breakfast, lunch and dinner together with the children, to talk of "kid things" with them (including their perceptions of their parents) and to play and teach each other together for more than a few hours. They were mannerly, fun, lively, smart and interesting. We liked each other a lot and had jolly times. Nice. I was getting to be the grandmother I liked to be. I have four grandchildren of my own but have never been in a rural, structured but totally open situation like this with them. Our times together have been pleasant but different—off to Gymboree, T-ball, art, swimming or acting lessons. Dinner with friends or at the clubhouse as the kids played with the other kids, or the kids playing computer games or watching a selected video.

It was strange to think that these good parents were younger than my children.

My morning walks sometimes produced unexpected pleasures, but also occasional sadness—like the time I ran across a haggard Murray, who had been up since 4:30. Poachers and predators were a very real threat in this country, and he had lost twenty-eight sheep. He had been out searching for evidence.

Another early morning, as I walked down the lane from the big old green wagon at the entrance to La De Da in my nightie and big hat, Murray and one of the boys came along on the tractor and waved as they went to the next field. He had done the family laundry and then went to turn over the rows of lucerne (alfalfa) so that it would dry evenly.

The last day of 1995 was a perfect midsummer day in the Great Karoo, with the hot Karoo wind blowing over everything. "The cypresses are stressed," Murray said. Too hard to get water to them. The great jacaranda trees rustled, seemingly unperturbed by the heat. New Year's Eve was quiet and lovely, the first time in fifty years that I can remember when there wasn't at least a glass of champagne around...and I could not remember being as content. I could barely stay awake until midnight even under the best of circumstances, so I left early to let them have a family quiet time and to do a little recollecting for myself. I was slightly awakened from a deep sleep by the distant clanging of wooden spoons on pots and pans, but quickly retreated to the first slumber of the new year.

We had been in town twice the previous week to get supplies and to do business, including once to take one of the employees' wives to the doctor. She was already a tad on the heavy side, but some allergy made her look like the Michelin Man. Her puffy eyes were swollen shut, and obviously she was in great discomfort. Her husband, Freia, was the oldest, most trusted and senior of the workers, and, clearly, real trust, respect and even affection existed between employer and employee. Automatically they got in the back of Murray's combi.

As we drove I kept asking myself "Has the check come?" Not that it was really any of my business. I hoped that after Murray got back from the bank I would be able to pick up information from a facial expression. While a good enough businessman, in my observation, Murray hated and distrusted banks, bankers, banking and a lot of things having to do with money. Mariette told me about the time that a beggar approached Murray soulfully with his hands out, reciting the customary line about needing to buy bread for his wife and children (as in the States, often really it's for wine). Murray dutifully gave him a fifty-cent piece, which would in fact buy some bread, and when the guy started complaining about how little it was, Murray promptly took the coin out of the beggar's hand and said, "I worked for this," and left.

The girls and I went to several shops looking for a new pocket calendar for me while the boys stuck with Murray and Mariette went to the market.

It was great fun for me to conspire with the children to get each a Magnum, a large, delicious, expensive Eskimo Pie-type ice cream bar on a stick. I had checked with Mariette as to whether or not this was okay, so she simply smiled when, after much protest about "you shouldn't do this" and "they're so expensive," the kids appeared chomping away excitedly. "Look what Auntie Martha got us!"

The whole family was driving to Cape Town the following Friday to take the girls back to boarding school. Murray would return that night and leave for business in Johannesburg the next day, which meant that he and I would have one night of overlap without the family. No way! According to his sensibilities, that would be totally improper. His plan was that the day they left in the combi, I would take the sedan and drive to town and spend the night at Matoppo House, now elegantly restored as a bed and breakfast, then come back Saturday and be driven to Graaff Reinet on Monday by the trusted helper, Freia. I told Murray that while I found Matoppo House charming, it really didn't seem necessary to move for just one night. Suddenly I realized that he was dead serious. "This is the right thing to do," he said firmly, "so that tongues won't wag."

I had to honor his sense of propriety, but it was all I could do to keep from laughing out loud. I repeated "Yes, so that tongues won't wag." It was settled. Besides, I could meet his mother and her new husband, who were up from the cape and would be staying there until he returned.

The next day we were to go to town to get a few things for the girls to take back to school. I appeared for breakfast dressed up enough for town but was then presented with a choice. Murray had to drive out to check the distant water tanks—did I want to go? I had driven out with him several times before and enjoyed it so much that now I jumped at the chance. I ran back to the big house, put on jeans, a tee shirt, boots and a big hat, grabbed my pack and was back in a flash. He was patiently sitting in the *bakkie*.

We drove past the kraal and the helpers' houses and waved at the black women, including the young woman we had seen in town on the first day. They were sweeping or tending their tidy gardens. All that was strictly women's work.

As a geologist in Wyoming and elsewhere I have opened and closed many a gate; but Murray's gentlemanliness wouldn't hear of it. He hopped out each time, drove through the gates and then jumped out again to close them. Several gates later he called to me to come to where he was. In his hands he had a huge tortoise, perhaps twenty inches from front to back. He turned it over and plucked a tick off a soft part above a hind leg and squashed the parasite between his fingers. "Those things are about the only real menace to these creatures," he said. Apparently it is a specialized tick that thrives in the Karoo because there are so many tortoises—five species.

Murray's eyes saw everything as we drove over the bumpy, sometimes nonexistent road. He suddenly stopped and cut the engine. "Look," he whispered and pointed at two little trees in the distance. I saw nothing unusual until a huge kudu (a large antelope with horns like corkscrews) bounded up the hill, followed by one, two, three, four. "Look," he said excitedly as he counted up to eleven. They were back, they were multiplying and there was room for the sheep and all of the animals. It was a wonderful sign of health and the prosperity of the land.

La De Da had more water in the form of natural springs—"fountains"—than many properties, and every few miles there would be an old silvercolored windmill and a large round concrete open-top tank about six feet tall and perhaps fifteen feet in diameter. A metal pipe led out of the bottom to a drinking trough, used by the wild animals as well as the domestic sheep and goats. As we drove from tank to tank Murray would point out good plants and toxic plants. He showed me different flocks of sheep and explained how they were separated and moved from one "pasture" to another through a gate that was left open or purposely closed. And he pointed out big and little animals (lots of the graceful springbok and occasionally even a little dikdik, the smallest of the antelope, sometimes less than three feet tall). The higher the sun rose, the hotter the day became. I was just observing, but he was working hard.

In each trough a ball float kept the water from overflowing. Periodically it got stuck or some other bit of maintenance was needed. He walked around each of the tanks looking for leaks and swept the troughs clean with a stiff brush to get rid of any moss or algae. One trough was overflowing profusely. He knelt down, stuck his arm into the trough and with a mighty tug yanked out a piece of rotted pipe. He would tell Freia, who would come out and replace it.

Murray was sweating profusely. I took a blue bandanna out of my pack and gave it to him. He wiped his brow. I said keep it. He thanked me. I hope he still uses it and knows how grateful I am for what I learned.

I met Iris for the first time one morning in the big house at La De Da. I had been working in my room and was walking down the hallway to the nearest bathroom to take a bath. (I could literally free-float in the gigantic bathtub.) At the far end of the hall was a tall, handsome young black woman with a scarf tied around her head and an apron—very plantation like. I walked down and introduced myself. With a small curtsey she said "Good day, madam" in impeccable English. "I hope I didn't disturb you, madam." She had been polishing the colossal kitchen at the far end of the house and had begun to sweep and polish the lovely hardwood floors in the corridors. They already looked cleaned and polished to me. Everything was "yes madam," "no madam," "yes madam." Clearly she was of the old school, or perhaps just incredibly shy. Because times were changing, I felt free to say, "Please don't keep calling me madam." She smiled and said "thank you madam" and then smiled broadly at what she had just said.

I saw Iris coming and going toward the kraal several times. The black people lived in several little houses beyond the wonderfully made old stone structure, which Murray and I passed as we drove out into the wilderness. I always waved, and timidly she waved and smiled. Later I realized that she would come to the kitchen in the small house and do the dishes after our meals.

The family left early Friday morning, and I left about noon for my big night at the fancy Matoppo House bed and breakfast in town. I stopped off at the Karoo National Park to visit a young woman named Liz who worked with the local farmers on the expansion of the park and who was in charge of ecological education. I wanted to give her my pin from the Sonoran Desert Alliance (an organization headquartered in Tucson that deals with the welfare of the Sonoran Desert on both sides of the Mexican border) and tell her that if she ever got discouraged to remember that there were people halfway around the world who believed in and were doing the same kind of work. She seemed very appreciative. Also, I wanted to look at the fascinating exhibits again and have luncheon in their cool dining room with picture windows looking out over bare mountains and valleys on a blazingly hot day.

A small group of investors had done a first-class job of restoring the historic Matoppo House. They had reproduced original types of wall paper and period furniture, quite European in feel, and converted the stables into attractive, comfortable rooms with expensive plumbing, big color TV, small refrigerators with cold milk for a cup of tea and queen-size beds.

I was greeted by the urbane manager, Marius, who understood my immediate need to get a telephone connection that would permit me to collect my e-mail. He brought a phone and a couple of different cords to my room. In South Africa, electrical cord connectors are different than in the U.S. Not only do they carry 220 volts, but they have a different shape, and the telephone cords differ further. In apartments and elsewhere the post office has installed meters on residential phones. One doesn't realize the full impact of this until making a long distance call and hearing the meter furiously whirring around.

I ended up in the main office doing my computer thing, but I'm quite certain that within a few days the next person with a laptop computer to occupy the room will have the proper wiring. During the cocktail hour, held beside the small freeform swimming pool, Marius introduced me to a charming German couple with whom I shared a table on the patio for an elegant gourmet supper and a lovely bottle of South African gran cru.

Murray's widowed mother had married a doctor from Cape Town. They were to arrive late that night and Murray had pre-arranged that we would have breakfast together. The charming elderly woman was smaller, more svelte and less intimidating than Aunt Clara Ford, and we seemed to have much to talk about. It really hit chords with me to be talking with the lady of the house who had lived, entertained and raised her children in that very house that I was staying in. I was acutely aware of the similarities between the old South Africa and old America—my "old America," meaning America in the thirties and forties.

Murray had come and gone by the time I arrived back at La De Da. Iris was cleaning the little house so that I could move in there the next day. It was really hot, so I invited her to sit down and "have a cool drink," a very South African expression for "Do you want some water?" or "Have a coke?" or something wet and cold.

She was no longer terribly shy, but I could tell she was think-ing over the appropriateness of my gesture before graciously accepting. I poured her some cold tea from the pitcher that was kept in the refrigerator.

We chit-chatted and I asked about where she had grown up.

"On a farm in the Transkai," she said, and she told me just how life was for her. With controlled emotion she told me of hiding in a shed and seeing her mother and father butchered when she was quite young. Clearly it was so stressful that I didn't ask her who killed them or why. We both were quiet for a spell.

"Tell me about your son," I said. She had been silent on the matter of a husband but lit up and like almost any attractive twenty eight-year-old with a nine-year-old son of whom she is very proud, told me how she was trying to raise him to be an honorable person. Murray had told me about some young black kid who had stolen meat from the freezer and how "they just don't have any sense of right and wrong and think somehow something is due them when it's not," even if he did give each family ten pounds of meat a week. Gradually it became harder and harder for me to believe it was Iris's boy, but who knew? The worlds were so far apart—part of the dilemma created all over the globe by differences in customs and attitudes and wealth.

I asked Iris bluntly if she could read. She said yes, so I gave her a copy of the draft of the new Constitution, which I had gotten in town and read thoroughly when I was at Matoppo House. It was to be finalized in May. I told her to study it and discuss it with her son, because this is their country too. She looked very pleased and said she would.

It was my last night in the big house. As the sun set and the generator droned in the distance, for the first time I was a tad apprehensive about being alone in the big house, I guess because of tales from Iris about the murder of her parents. But soon the feeling passed.

Early Sunday morning I moved into the little house with Iris's help. When we finished she said she would be right back. She was going "over there," nodding in the direction of the black people's cottages. I must have looked puzzled. She said apologetically "To go to the toilet." I frowned and nodded her toward the one in the house.

I thanked her for helping me move and gave her a five-rand coin to buy her son a present. She seemed truly thrilled, and without thinking gave me an African handshake, which I could do quite well by then. She seemed startled at what she had done. I smiled and gave her a hug.

Happy as I was, this wonderful spell did have to end eventually. Actually I was glad to have some time to myself and decided to go for a walk. As I started down the wide dirt road, the big old yellow Labrador apparently didn't want me to go alone and shortly was by my side. I talked to him and he listened as we went out past what was called the "family of windmills," five big silver structures with slowly turning blades pumping precious water into five cement tanks. It was hot and oh so still and peaceful on the blistering dry ground of the Karoo.

When we finally returned, I gave the dog the water in which I had hard-boiled some eggs. It had calcium, and also one tries not to waste a drop of water. And then I gave him more. The young dog came over to drink. I held him back for a while. They both seemed to understand. Amazing how they do that.

The old South Africa was a union of two Boer-dominated republics, the Transvaal and the Orange Free State, and two

British colonies, Natal and the Cape, before it became a republic on May 31, 1961. A compromise over the location of the capital was necessary. The solution, three capitals. Cape Town,
former capital of the large Cape Province, became the legislative capital; Bloemfontein, former capital of the Orange Free
State, became the judicial capital; Pretoria, the former capital of
the Transvaal (and in the mid-1800s, capital of the Boer Republic) now serves as the administrative capital of the republic, still
using the handsome old Union Buildings. The Union Buildings, which sit atop a high hill above terraced gardens, were really a single building with two wings, which supposedly represented the two official languages, English and Afrikaans, which
existed at the time of the Union, 1919 through 1961.

One can't speak of the "old South Africa" without talking
about one of its most famous, historic and interesting cities, Pretoria, still a Boer city in many respects.

Because Johannesburg, commonly known as "Joburg,"
financial capital and largest city in South Africa, has quite a rep-
utation for street crime, I decided to stay in Pretoria, about forty kilometers to the north. After an all-night bus ride from Namibia, I had to change buses at the Johannesburg Rotunda (bus
terminal). After I collected my luggage I approached two large,
uniformed bus officials standing by the bus and asked where to
go to get the bus to Pretoria. One of them turned angrily and
said rudely "Don't interrupt. Can't you see we're talking? And
it's very important." As he turned his back I was about to say
"'Scuse me, I thought you were here to serve the public," but
thought better of it and walked to a policeman, also black, who
had seen the whole thing. With a shake of his head and a mild
apology, he pointed to another gate.

Pretoria was my first extended stay anywhere after my
month in Cape Town and then a month in Namibia. I found the
town quiet (most of the time), charming, historic and very conservative but reasonably friendly, although I began to overhear
really rude comments about "those people," meaning homosexuals. To many South Africans, Pretoria is stodgy, if not just plain
boring, but I had a wonderful time.

Late December is summer in South Africa, and just a few
blossoms lingered from the spectacular spring event in October

in Pretoria, when 85,000 jacaranda trees burst into a mass of gorgeous bloom, variously described as purple, lavender or periwinkle. In early December, anyone who was able has left Pretoria and Joberg for the Christmas holidays, which is also like summer vacation. So, while there was still lots of activity, Pretoria was pleasantly uncrowded for me.

I had asked my newspaper friends in Namibia for an adequate, relatively inexpensive place to stay, and with some apprehension they suggested the Hotel 224. "Lots of press people stay there, but you might not like it," they said.

I was puzzled by the comment but ignored it until I got to the front desk to register. Standing at the end of the counter was a hard-faced young lady with bleached-blond hair, smoking. She wore knee boots, a little strip of cloth around her waist that she must have thought resembled a skirt, and a tight (very tight) "blouse" of sleazy material.

The young black helper-boy provided by the front desk to assist with my luggage was certainly courteous, but when we couldn't get the closet door open in my small, dark room, I was surprised to learn that he didn't know how to use the phone to call about a key for it. Almost always closets or armoires, even ones in homes, have locks. I'm relatively certain that he was illiterate, albeit good natured. We agreed that he should go get a key for the closet. He returned so quickly that I could hardly believe he had run down and up three flights of stairs. We both fiddled with the lock, and as he finally got it to turn he said "This thing is really fucked up." I tried not to smile, looked as non-committal as I could, tipped him well and thought of my WorldTeach friend Michael, who had reminded me one must be careful about swearing in another language.

The hotel was wonderfully located for exploring the city. As I wandered around town, I was very much reminded of the older parts of Washington, D.C. with its embassies, parks, boulevards, monuments and public buildings and grounds. Again a déjà vu for me. Fresh out of college I had moved to Washington to begin my work with the U.S. Geological Survey.

At the end of a rose garden park I discovered the American embassy. There was nothing "old Africa" about it—a huge cement fortress with slit windows, surrounded by wide lawns, several layers of high fences and very controlled entrances with armed guards. Even with my passport and gray hair I had to fill out questionnaires and be frisked twice before being permitted to look up some stuff in the library.

I was unaffected by the goings-on at the hotel for the first couple of nights until a rowdy bunch of young people moved to my floor and partied noisily day and night. The managment seemed unconcerned.

A short distance from the hotel, at the base of the manicured hills and terraced gardens on which the old Union Buildings sit, I had passed by the YWCA, an attractive fenced-in three-story brick building, which had a small sign saying fifty-five rand (about fourteen dollars) per night, which was about a third of what I was paying at the hotel. My last distinct memory of a "Y" was forty years ago when I had just moved to San Francisco and stayed at a Y for a few days until I could get an apartment. The Pretoria Y was not appreciably different, although Christianity in the new South African Pretoria seemed much more intense than I remembered it from 1950's San Francisco.

Fortunately, the population of permanent, religiously devout (proselytizing) residents was diminished because almost everyone had gone home for the holidays. Living there would leave me with more money to travel and a place to leave my luggage for short trips. So I accepted the spartan room and terms and moved in. In my notes I keep finding reference to those "canvas sheets." The texture was a little rough on the cheeks and elbows, but they were certainly clean.

One of the things I wanted to do was go to the northern border of South Africa to see the Limpopo River. When I was a child, one of my fondest memories of a fascinating, complex mother was the verve with which she read "...the great gray green greasy Limpopo River..." from Kipling's "How the Elephant Got Its Trunk," one of the *Just-So Stories.* It seemed to be one of her very favorites, and hence I heard it often. For years it never occurred to me that the Limpopo River was something other than a rich, rolling passage in a dramatic tale. It was a boundary, shared with Zimbabwe.

After so many years of drought, it had begun to rain heavily, murderously in some places, especially in the north and east of

South Africa. The first news I saw as I sat in the lounge of the Y were dramatic shots of the devastating floods on the Limpopo River, which threatened to tear out the new bridge to Zimbabwe. So I scratched that plan.

Every major city has a tourist information center, a place that should definitely be checked out by visitors because of the wealth of information it provides. In the lobby of the Pretoria tourist office there was a coffee shop, a travel agency and several other business. At the far end, a very colorful geometric mural caught my eye. The classical Ndebele patterns formed a backdrop for Tebu Tours, which turned out to be one of the most enriching mechanisms I could have found. The owners, Tebello and Busi, a very handsome young black couple, he part historian and professional guide, she an excellent salesperson and business manager, provided "cross-cultural tours." While there have always been black entrepreneurs, since apartheid was lifted just a few short years earlier they had much to learn rapidly about competing in a still white-dominated industry.

It is one thing to visit Soweto in a van or bus full of visitors, even with a black driver, and another to drive with two other people in a private car with a black man who knows every inch of the territory and will freely and articulately talk of history and politics, black and white, rich and poor and anything else you want to ask about. Tebello first took us to the Africa Museum in Johannesburg to trace the history of the country, especially of the black people, and of how Soweto had come into being. The museum has many unique exhibits, including one on the history of jazz in Africa and a life-sized model of a shanty town. One small shelter, just a few feet square, had a dirt floor, sleeping mats, a tiny stove and tattered burlap walls and "roof." "This is just like the one my father used to live in," Tebello said contemplatively.

In Soweto, mostly a huge, dreary, littered, treeless, dusty sprawling area with people, graffiti and abandoned cars everywhere, we would drive long distances and Tebello would answer the questions of a young Swiss guy and me. Some neighborhoods were squalid; some, including the one where Bishop Tutu and the Mandelas had lived (and Winnie still lives) were more elegant—groomed brick houses and some landscaping. Nobody really knew Soweto's population exactly, but an estimated population of about three million people of color lived here. Soweto, which is an acronym for South West Territories, is one of the areas outside of Johannesburg where the black people who worked in town (or in the nearby gold mines) were permitted to live. In earlier days the miners who mined the gold reefs surrounding Johannesburg lived in all-male and racially segregated company barracks. En route back to Pretoria we dropped off the Swiss guy at the huge soccer arena. He wanted to get tickets for a big game that night and assured us that he would be able to get back to Pretoria by himself.

Notes in my laptop computer dated December 16, 1995, read:

> There were fewer people on the streets when I went out for a walk and some offices appeared closed. Today is/ was some sort of national holiday. Neither the new temp at the front desk (who doesn't seem overly bright) nor the young, big, thick girl [Boers tend to have a big, blocky and rather featureless stature] who was heading upstairs even seemed aware that it was a holiday. I looked at the date on the calendar in the office and still couldn't tell much except that it was the Day of the Vow, whatever that is. At the mall the lady at the ice cream store didn't know. She said she thought it was something like Children's Day.

Later when watching the eight o'clock news in the TV room I asked an older woman who did some bookeeping for the Y about the Day of the Vow. She said, very abruptly, it was the Day of the Covenant when less than 500 Boers defeated over 12,000 Zulu warriors at Blood River, having vowed to build a church if they survived.

"You know how this new government has changed everything. I think they are calling it the Day of Reconciliation or something like that," she said and went back to glaring at the tube.

"You know how this new government is," is a phrase that some white people say often, but my observation is that they only say it to other white people. Obviously deprecating, but just sort of "Oh, well."

Several days later, when I visited the Vooertrekker Monument, a cube of granite 130 feet on a side that commemorates the Great Trek in 1836, I began to understand more about the Boer point of view. In the basement of the monument was a granite slab, the "Altar of Sacrifice," engraved with the words "We for thee, South Africa." At exactly noon on December 16, the Day of the Vow (Covenant), a ray of light from a slit in the roof focuses on the inscription for a short time.

I had previously visited many landmarks and interesting places around the town, like Melrose House, where Lord Kitchner and other Englishmen strategized the second Anglo-Boer war at the turn of the century. It is steeped in the "British view" of the Boers. The well-preserved Victorian house has much original wallpaper, original furniture and knickknacks. It felt odd that my foot might be falling on the exact spot that those historic people had walked—not that I think what the British did was wonderful, like killing the Boers' livestock, burning their crops and setting up cruel concentration camps, where women and children were brutalized. The Brits won, and the peace treaty was signed at that very house.

The Boers, Afrikaners who took the Bible literally, were descendants of original Dutch and French settlers. They went cross-country to escape British rule. They hadn't really gotten on very well together, a fact that culminated in the Anglo-Boer wars to set up their own country, after defeating the Zulus at Blood River. But in Hollywood fashion, if you turn the camera in the opposite direction, instead of seeing brave white guys heading into the wilderness, as depicted in the monument, you, as a black person who had already been squeezed down from further north by other black people…well, you might perceive a slow moving white cannon ball coming directly at your head.

The huge bas reliefs around the interior walls of the monument were reminiscent of the American covered wagon treks across the continent to the west, except that the Boers were so clearly religious and properly dressed. The museum across the way had the same story as the friezes, but done in amazing tapestries of colorful, intricate needlework.

Many Afrikaners were still believers in the separation and superiority of their racial purity, and a small but organized and vocal number still actively seek a separate white nation, which doesn't exactly fit into the vision of those in authority in the new South Africa. It will be interesting to see what happens at the monument, which serves as a sacred meeting place for believers. My view was that the tapestries should be displayed and seen by everyone as the incredible works of art that they were.

Everything, the displays of wagons and tools and guns, reminded me so much of our great westward migration. The third grade at the Angell School in Ann Arbor, Michigan, seat of the University of Michigan from which I would later graduate, was my first encounter with the type of teacher who is far more interested in form than in substance—Miss Chapin. I can visualize her now and will use her name because she must be long gone. She publicly humiliated me for not having a cover on my lengthy report (lengthy for the third grade) on "The Westward Migration." I quickly painted a pointed mountain and told her it was Pike's Peak. And I wasn't the least bit sorry when the wet paint dribbled on her desk.

I understand the "colonialization" of our West differently now, and seeing the similarities with the trekkers enhanced my insights. I am very American and love the idea of bursting forth into the beautiful wilderness. I like the idea of sweating and enduring the elements in the American West, stories of hewing your logs, building your cabin, planting your crops, etc. But we did the same things to our Native Americans that the white people did to Native Africans.

I am proud to trace my roots way back into American history, but I am not afraid to deal with the injustices and cruelties of the past. My father used to announce proudly that I had three verifiable routes to becoming a member of the Daughters of the American Revolution, the famous/infamous DAR.

A once-famous but largely forgotten American artist in the thirties and forties, Betsy Graves Reyneau, did a series of portraits of famous American Negroes, as they were called in those days, including boxer Joe Louis, still a much-admired figure in South Africa, and a jewel of a portrait of George Washington Carver that hangs in the Smithsonian Institution in Washington, D.C.

Betsy, an old friend of my mother's, also did a portrait of the famous singer Marion Anderson, the first black to sing at the Metropolitan Opera in New York. Anderson was refused the right to present a concert in DAR facilities in Washington simply because she was black. With the help of the president's wife, Eleanor Roosevelt, and others, she was permitted to sing on the steps of the Lincoln Memorial, overlooking a huge audience in the same spaces that were later filled with large crowds honoring various blacks, including Martin Luther King. The mid-nineties "Million Man March," held in those same spaces, was an event viewed with puzzlement by most white South Africans I talked with. They had never seen so many black American males at one time and, like many white Americans, had mixed feelings about the organizer, Louis Farakan. Farakan was famous in South Africa for his anti-Semitic and black-power speeches, and yet the rally seemed to be about personal responsibility and reconciliation—dominant themes of the Mandela government.

The thunderheads were building, and it was a long way back to the freeway where I had gotten off the bus to go to the Voortrekker Monument. So I approached a woman with two young boys who appeared pleasant and agreeable and asked if she was driving back to town. She kept saying "shaim"...like it's a shame that there is no bus, it's a shaim (shame) about this or that. Rather limited, but nice. She was very Afrikaans, a typical suburban housewife taking her sister's two kids out. They'd been to the monument numerous times but not to Melrose House or any number of other places that also are very historic. She didn't even know about them. She only knew about Boer things and seemed unconscious about the relationship between old and new South Africa. I gratefully accepted a ride back to downtown Pretoria.

CHAPTER 6

THE SHEEP, THE GOATS
AND THE WILD THINGS

Amazing how attuned to this country I'm becoming. I know my geography fairly well. I am concerned about the rain, too much and too little, about the fires, about political events and history, etc. And I care about a lot of people.

From week twelve, Pretoria

The farm La De Da was an example of the end of an era—the old South Africa. But there is much more to say about it as a physical place, a sheep farm, and the role of this lifestyle in the transitions to new ways in southern Africa. Wool and mohair are major exports from southern Africa, so sheep farming is a big deal. In South Africa several types of the black-faced Dorper and thick wooly Merino sheep dominate. In Southern Namibia, kar-akul sheep dominate because of their ability to survive the high, hot, dry, windy, freezing aridity; well worth the effort because of the valuable qualities of the pelts.

Sheep meat (we call it lamb, they call it mutton) is another major industry. Many countries claim to have the best eating lamb, but I have never had better, and happily I had a lot of it. Many of the grazing plants in the Karoo are aromatic, so the meat is delicately "pre-seasoned."

A number of poisonous plants do exist, and if not eradicated in one way or another would take over and render the land unfit for grazing. I had read that during the periods of conquest, annexation and just plain stealing of tribal lands in southern Africa, the "reservations" where the natives were compelled to live were essentially unfit for their cattle or sheep because the poisonous species were very abundant. Because of this and the scarcity of water, the land was hardly "choice real estate." We did the same things to many American Indian tribes. The land was viewed as worthless—until uranium and other minerals were discovered there. Then, although the natives usually received money for mineral royalties, the mining practices of large companies really poisoned the land and water. Minerals of all kinds, including uranium, do exist on farms in southern Africa, including La De Da. Diamond and gold mining began after discovery on farmlands.

Sheep farms tend to be very large because the land supports so few living things per acre. The hectare (equivalent to about two and a half acres) is the unit of land measurement there, but by any measure, the farms are huge in South Africa and especially huge in Namibia—some in the tens of thousands of hectares. In southern Namibia a home can be three hours by dirt road from the nearest off-the-main-road burg where a bus passes by its crossroads a few times a week, often late at night or before dawn. Many children from very remote areas attend boarding school for the upper grades, and become generally very well educated. But the children of workers are even more isolated than farm children in other parts of the world.

I was fortunate to spend time on two different sheep farms in the Great Karoo, La De Da, near Beaufort West, and Spring Grove near Graaff Reinet. Granted, many of the people I met were "pre-selected" by being friends of friends, but my experiences as a stranger and a foreigner were almost universally experiences of extraordinary hospitality.

On both farms, it was the same industry (the raising of animals for wool and meat), and same kinds of people—handsome, rugged, young, smart, conservative, aggressive and hard working. Both had young children, both were tied to a city by history and relatives. Both farms were near the same latitude (about 32° 30' S), although Spring Grove is at a much higher elevation and considerably more remote. Both are about as Karoo as you can get, both have pigs, goats, Dorper sheep, Merino sheep, incredible varieties of wild animals and long histories of being held and worked by white farmers.

Both farms had been ravaged by the drought and brought to the brink of bankruptcy. La De Da was sold. Spring Grove held on because the owner, Jan Piet Steynberg, got involved in road maintenance and construction to help make payments. Similarities abound, but interesting differences enriched my understanding of farms, farming, people and southern Africa.

The nine years without rain had ruined many farms and farm families and industries, and coupled with international economic sanctions imposed because of apartheid, vital parts of the economy were brought to the fringes of disaster. Prosperous citrus farmers in the north ripped out thousands of hectares of trees as they died off. That the drought played a role in hastening the demise of the unacceptable political system seems a bizarre kind of poetic justice; but the innocent suffered with the guilty.

The foreman, Freia, and his family had driven me from La De Da to Graaff Reinet through vast expanses of the Karoo. Clearly we were gaining altitude along the way, and the mountains were becoming more rugged. Per my agreement with Murray, we filled up with petrol and I bought a few treats for the children and for each "a pie," a common meal or snack consisting of a closed pastry shell filled with meat. Freia was a good driver, but didn't often venture so far from home. He dropped me off at the elegantly restored old Drostdy Hotel (built in 1806) in Graaff Reinet. Originally, it says in a brochure, this was the seat of local government of an "outpost of white civilization in a barren and untamed country." Hester Steynberg picked me up in the elegant gardens. We had a cup of coffee and quickly discovered that we had lots of interests in common.

Graaff Reinet is a "Williamsburg" kind of place, full of monuments, Cape Dutch buildings and distinctive Karoo houses. We walked from one historic building to another, including one with a kitchen floor made entirely of peach pits, ending up at Lena Steynberg's house. Lena, Hester's mother-in-law, is very elderly but spry and loves having her son, Jan Piet (J.P. for short), Hester and their children visit and stay over when they come to town from the family farm, Spring Grove.

The house, built in 1902 by Lena's grandparents, has the highest ceilings I have ever seen in a regular residence—maybe twenty feet—with a yellowwood molding about a yard down from the ceiling to hang picture wires from, and another about four feet up from the reddish plank floors to be a furniture rub guard. The furniture was mulberry, stinkwood, yellowwood and the various other stunning South African woods that are becoming scarce because of over-harvesting.

I was struck by the incongruity of old and new: Hester's powerful computer and printer stood on an ancient desk in my bedroom. Although trained as a nurse with specialties in mid-wifery and psychiatry and having practiced for years, she used the computer mainly to keep various farm records and to teach other people bookkeeping, spreadsheets, and so forth.

Another striking anomaly was Hester's casual comment that half of Graaff Reinet was on Prozac because there was a doctor who prescribed it for just about everything. She sensed my eyebrows rising when she said "half," so she smiled and said "a lot."

The next day I entertained myself walking to the historic places while she did business (J.P. had already gone back to Spring Grove). The following morning we left early for the farm, taking a slight detour to the top of a nearby mountain with 360-degree views. Spandau-kop, an isolated mountain whose top was often above the fog that filled the valley that contained Graaff Reinet. You can't see a picture of the town without seeing this mountain symbol. In the opposite direction the breath-taking view of Desolation Valley, not unlike our Death Valley, but absolutely empty. Near Graaff Reinet itself there were two distinct patches of shanty towns, one for blacks and one for coloureds, now called mixed-race people. In my country, we used to call black people colored people, but fashions in naming change over the years. These people just don't mix, I was told, and repeatedly I had heard of friction between these groups all over the country. "Who needs more strife?" I thought to myself.

Hester and I drove quite far out of town, then turned off the main road and drove for perhaps an hour or so on deteriorating roads through absolutely gorgeous country. Down in a deep green valley below was a large white farmhouse and outbuild-ings. She said that it was the last one before theirs, and very so-berly added that the wife had been murdered—her throat slit so brutally it had almost severed her head from her body. Tales of other murders nearby gradually seeped out during my stay, some of them incredibly grisly, like the one about a woman who had disappeared and been found much later stuffed in an aard-vark burrow.

We climb to about 6,000 feet at the base of a rugged moun-tain called Nadau, composed of thick flat-lying sandstone beds and steep cliffs. It reminded me of the country around Sonoita, Arizona.

At the high fence surrounding the house, I was introduced to the rotweiler, who Hester assured me was a creampuff—but she warned me *not* to go out at night because they released an-other rotweiler that was strictly a guard dog (I could fill in the blanks: "he will tear you limb from limb.")

I was introduced to the two attractive young boys who smiled and stood politely but said nothing except a faltering "Welcome, Auntie Martha." Hester explained that they only spoke Afrikaans, although the older boy did understand quite a bit of English.

Then without notice I was startlingly introduced to Merkie, a young meerkat, a prairie dog-like animal about ten inches long, who from nowhere leapt onto one of the boys' shoulders and then to mine. He was carefully peeled away, and shot off in the opposite direction. Usually one sees meerkats in endearing almost human poses, standing up on their hind legs with straight backs, braced by a thin tail, front legs poised in delicate, very human-like positions and looking diligently in all direc-tions. They are a swiftly moving small mass of energy when they aren't resting in one's hands or on one's shoulder nibbling one's ear lobe.

As we sat on the veranda "having a cool drink" we looked at old picture albums, a clear record of a ten-year evolution of the plain farmhouse. There was no grass or gardens, just dirt where now are colorful, lush and interesting displays. Everywhere there were beds of flowers, and a little bridge crossing an artifi-cial creek in the grassy front yard. The setting was spectacular, and a beautiful place had been enhanced by vigorous, careful work of this couple.

During the past decade they had added a large family room facing the mountain cliffs, with polished flagstone flooring and cobbles of the local stone facing a large open fireplace—it did snow and get very cold there in the winter. Lots of artwork, including oriental things collected by several generations, and an intricate carving of the Last Supper from a large piece of wild olive that had been done by J.P.'s grandfather as a school project.

The home was also definitely a little boy's home, with pieces of puzzles and Legos and Erector Sets and tools and projects, all of which would be neatly put away by bedtime.

One morning I walked far out in back, past a large cage with a shelter at one end where they kept the "naughty goat," a sturdy young male who was determined to mix up the genetics of every animal it could find. Large patches of grass around the generator shed were kept mowed low by sheep. Beyond the windmills were the trim little houses of the workers near the edge of the alfalfa (lucerne) fields, the rough natural Karoo beyond. I was reminded of several ranches I had visited in our own West that were similarly laid out.

A large, round concrete water tank with a ladder propped to climb to the top was used as a swimming pool by everyone. The farm children in such remote areas become the playmates of the owners' children, and their "problems" are those of children, not of race.

That night J.P. invited me to see what he was doing on the computer in a very comfortable library/study. Obviously he could turn the power—the generator—on and off, but it was more economical to work while it was on the regular timer sequence. He was making final entries in a complex spreadsheet because the inspector was coming the next day to classify some of his sheep, a special kind of Merino.

The grading was done every six months for the quality of the wool, the general health of the animals, and the presumed quality of the meat, all of which had enormous implications in terms of value of the flock. AA is the best grade. Lowercase letters are used for animals less than a year old.

The inspector, a tall, lean man resembling a rich Texas rancher, arrived very early the next morning. The workers had all of the animals ready. The man really knew his business, and he had looked over these animals since they were born, so it only took about an hour. And then, naturally, we all sat on the veranda and had a cool drink. J.P.'s sheep were all AA or aa, and the genealogy of every animal was stored in the computer. Handy, yes, but the principles of grading and record keeping had been used for generations.

My father used to take us to farms when I was a child and I kept seeing and feeling things that I hadn't experienced for years. I do think people are richer for having had experiences on farms, experiences that many American children will never have.

J.P. went off to work every day, but always came home for a hearty luncheon—typical farm routine. Sometimes he would come home in mid-afternoon, turn on the generator and watch the cricket matches. I teased him about being the only farmer in South Africa who planned his work schedule around the cricket matches. On certain days the power would be turned on in the afternoon for an hour so that the children could watch selected television shows.

The midday meal was the big meal in most of South Africa. On farms like Spring Grove, they used home grown vegetables and meat. Savory simple food was prepared on the most impressive stove I had ever seen. An ever-burning gigantic yellow enameled iron stove, which must have weighed at least half a ton, was in its own room off the kitchen, because there was always warmth. It had several ovens, special lids to control heat when it was not in use and was fueled with chunks of anthracite coal, which I hadn't seen since I was a kid, when occasionally I would help shovel coal into our furnace in wintery Detroit.

A large pot of coffee was always kept on the back of the stove, because in midmorning and midafternoon the workers took breaks. I had observed that many South Africans actually prefer coffee to tea, but it was still called teatime.

Meals were conversational times, not just eat and run. Discussions were of great interest to me, and because they didn't often have houseguests "from America," there was lots of information we could pass back and forth. Several times we had long political talks and got down to some deep feeling about white farmers versus black farmers and related subjects. There had been lots of violence on both sides in this area, more than I had noticed elsewhere, including marauders and the seemingly gratuitous murders of white women.

The large gun safe in my bedroom was locked (by law), but I asked to see what was inside. Matter of factly, J.P. unlocked it and took out a heavy AK-47 type automatic weapon which I could hardly lift, let alone aim. The shells were about the size of my middle finger, and the gun was designed to shoot continuously as long as the trigger was depressed. It would take very little time to cut a person in half—which, I guess, was the idea.

The government now provided guns to the farmers in this area, and without notice an inspector could stop by to make sure they were locked up. There were gun safes in other rooms as well.

Another time we had good chats about being Jewish. Since before the beginning of the twentieth century, Jews had been an important part of South African history, in traditional work like trade and finance, and, in South Africa, especially in various aspects of the diamond industry. There were Jewish museums in most big cities, including a prominent one in Cape Town. But for generations there had been farmers who may have had very diluted blood lines but still carried Jewish names forward.

Like many South Africans, Hester had travelled quite a bit in Europe and Israel as a young college student, but said that it was in Spain that she had begun to develop her thoughts on the desirability of not mixing cultures. My sense was that she, like those of us who struggle with complex alternatives, was still developing her thoughts. I was honored that she would even talk with me so honestly. There was a map nearby, and she was assigning territory to various cultures. And mixed cultures went to "gray areas."

Things got a little complicated when I raised the point of where to put people who were excluded by their own culture—like gay people, who were not really accepted in some societies. In all cultures there are taboos and exclusions and outcasts. "They all would be assigned to some other gray area," she thought, but clearly that wouldn't work because we were running out of territory. I guess we both were still thinking.

Now that the inspections were done, it was time for shearing. As a kid I had seen fast, efficient shearing with electric clippers on a ranch in Idaho; but it wasn't since the mid-1960s in Iceland that I had seen shearing by hand with those old-fashioned pointed steel clippers that periodically are brought to razor sharpness on a handheld whetstone.

The worker took a dried kernel of corn from a small bucket that had a certain number of kernels known only to J.P. and grabbed another sheep that was hustled in by a young boy. The man locked a sheep between his legs and clipped until the sheep was almost naked, and slapped it on the rear to shoo it out the door. It was a little disconcerting to me that sometimes the thin layer of snowy white fleece was spotted with bright red blood, but everyone assured me that it was superficial. My city-slicker mentality was still bothered. The corn kernel provided a count, but everybody knew everybody else's count anyhow.

J.P. stood at a large wooden frame with small rollers on top in the middle of a stone barn overlooking four workers who did the actual shearing. Amazingly the wool came off the sheep as a single piece, if the clippers were as skilled as these men were. He took the wool over to J.P.'s table where J.P. rolled it back and forth. He broke off pieces of different qualities and threw them into separate tan fiberglass bags that resembled burlap. Little scraps fell through the rollers, which were heavily coated with years of lanolin deposits. This sorting is critical because bales were randomly sampled by the wool brokers in Port Elizabeth, and the slightest deviation or imperfection—like the occasional naturally occurring single stiff, almost plastic-like hair—could cause the entire bale to be classified at a much lower rank and value.

The difficult work of shearing went on day after day. We, the women and children, did "women and children things," like feeding the baby goats and other animals, and taking long walks to some of the beautiful sites on the property. We swept a path in front of us with a long stick as we walked through the knee-high lovely green field of lucerne to frighten away the cobras and black mambo snakes—a scary thought to me.

95

A creek that had been dry for years now had its great water-fall back, and it was thrilling to see several rare antelope and the handsome kudu with its corkscrew horns scamper up past segments of black PV pipe away from the waterfall as we approached. Hester explained that they had had to run a series of pipes far, far up the mountain to tap into springs during the drought to even get drinking water.

Almost as scary as the deadly snakes was crossing a muddy enclosure where there were more pigs than usual because of the recent birth of a litter. I remembered how dangerous pigs could be, and my thoughts were confirmed as Hester quickly shepherded the boys to the next gate and motioned me to hurry as she held tight to a big stick and kept a wary eye on a lumbering sow, which could run very fast when it wanted to.

Hester sewed beautifully and was making new school clothes for the boys. She also spent lots of time on the phone with friends and with people who were learning about computers and bookkeeping. The boys and I would play games and teach each other words. They were fascinated with my laptop computer, so we had a few lessons with it.

One morning we stopped by the barn to watch J.P. and the shearing. He was talking to "the hide man," an oddly specialized profession that filled a definite need in the livestock business. The hide man, who went to school with J.P., apparently had had some major illness that had taken a chip off at least one of his marbles; but he was competent to be a hide man. The hides from all the animals, wild and domestic, that have been slaughtered during the last few month were stored in a small building near the barn. The hide man bossed his one worker officiously. The worker held up a stiff hide, the hide man looked at it, felt it and wrote down a figure in a little notebook. The worker went over to the pickup truck and tossed the hide on top of the already overloaded accumulation from visits to other farms. The worker went back to the shed and came out with two more hides. They were big and heavy, but that was his job.

Half an hour and perhaps forty hides later, the hide man retreated to add up his figures and drew J.P. aside to give him some paper money. Hester said it was essentially nothing, but it was better than throwing the hides away; and besides it gave this guy and his worker a job.

Courtesy demanded that the hide man be offered a cool drink. He ended up inviting himself to luncheon and talking a lot about his incredibly racist attitudes, about "how dumb, stupid and lazy his nigger helper is." His comments became extremely nasty and bordered on violent until J.P. tactfully changed the subject. Later Hester whispered that he was "full of hot air and just talks like that," but that he was really harmless; somewhat disconcerting, though. J.P. went back to the shearing barn, and finally Hester, the kids and I retired for a nap while the hide man sat still in a rocking chair on the veranda, talking softly to himself.

Late one afternoon J.P. came home early and suggested that we drive out to try to find the black springbok. Apparently two had been spotted on the property during the last few months. The springbok, one of the loveliest and most abundant of the many antelope, was delicate, beautifully marked with a dark band of smooth hair parallel to the backbone on each side of the shaded beige pelt, and a true joy to watch move. There was something about the way the hips were put together that let it "spring" across a road or a fence or just bound across the plain. I had only heard about black ones, and apparently they were rare.

Many farmers had a weather eye toward the tourist industry, because they were acutely aware that visitors are part of the future economic health of the country, and they, the farmers, often owned what people wanted to see. In the back of J.P.'s mind was building up a herd of black springbok, which could become a real attraction. A famous zebra park already existed on the other side of the mountain.

"It's kind of a rough ride, but would you like to go?" he asked me hesitantly. Without thinking I quoted one of my son's favorites lines: "Does a bear crap in the woods?" He burst into his characteristic broad smile and said, "That's good, that's good."

He said it would be more comfortable to ride standing up in the back of the pickup holding onto the special rail than to sit in the cab, so the kids and I braced ourselves. At first we bumped over what it took a little generosity to call a road, but gradually that deteriorated. Periodically we would stop, he would stick his head out of the cab and point out some rare plant or point to a bird or an animal, once to a cobra crossing the road.

The ride became rougher and rougher—white knuckles, including on the boys. We drove around the larger rocks and bushes, but my breath stopped as we slowed down and I heard the grinding of gears as we headed straight down an incredibly steep bank into a river. It looked like the nose of the truck would be buried in the water, but with a crunch we churned across and up the seemingly impossibly steep opposite bank. But we made it.

We were in the middle of nowhere. Pristine green and gray rolling horizontal surfaces and tan and brown cliffs took on the blush of a sinking sun. So empty, and yet so full. We stopped and all just silently looked at the mountains surrounding us. J.P. got out, surveyed and, suddenly putting his finger to his lips, pointed to a distant ravine. By the time I got focused, I just saw a dark animal rump disappearing. Wow. When the silence was broken I asked, "If the black ones sometimes have white babies, how can you increase the number of black ones?" The ironic answer was a matter of fact: "Shoot out the white lambs."

By the time we got back to the farm road, the sun was dropping below the horizon. It felt like we were driving on a freeway.

The next day was the last of the shearing and the sealing of the five-foot-high bales of various grades of wool for shipment to the wool co-op in Port Elizabeth, a large industrial town on the Indian Ocean. A little free time, for a change. The family had planned a short vacation trip to the seaside to do some shopping and errands before school resumed. And thrill of thrill for the boys, to stay at a real motel on the waterfront.

Again I was faced with a transportation problem, or perhaps I should say "lack of public transportation problem," something that South Africa needs to improve before they solicit hoards of tourists. So we loaded up the combi and headed south. I was to be picked up at the airport by a friend to go to exclusive Jeffrey's Bay on the coast of the Indian Ocean, which, I was told, was the only community left in South Africa with an all-white local government.

But first, happily, P.J. had arranged for me to go to BKB, the Farmers' Brokers (Co-op) Ltd. in the heart of the large and very industrial city of Port Elizabeth. The special building where auctions and activities related to sheep from all over the country were held, and the large building across the street, the wool/mohair co-op, were closed for the last few days of the Christmas holidays. But P.J.'s old schoolmate and business colleague at the co-op, the Chief Mohair Technical official, had offered to show me and the little boys through while the parents went on errands.

The co-op comprised eight acres, three stories of cement floors and walls and rooms under one roof in one huge building. Most of the three-foot-wide roller belts flush with the floor were still. Occasionally one would start up and move a few of the gigantic fiberglass bales (like the ones J.P. had filled at the barn) to the other end of the building or to a huge chute where they would fall to the floor below. There was lots of empty space, because except for certain activities, mainly to do with mohair (which is very different from wool), the operation was closed down for the holidays. Some walls were lined with bales of wool or somewhat smaller bales of mohair.

A peculiar looking, one-purpose machine had a clamping device and a three-inch-diameter barrel that punched right through the center of the bales and extracted cores. The fate of sheep farmers all over the country rest with the analysis of that core, which was why J.P. was so meticulous about sorting his wool. The bale was graded on the various tests conducted on the core, like a test for any of those stiff little plastic-like hairs J.P. had shown me. The bale was also tested for kinkiness, fineness, color, cleanliness, etc. Then bales of the same grade were slit open and emptied into bins big enough to park two cars side by side. Wool buyers from all over the world came to bid on the contents of those bins—a vital part of the South African economy.

Thus ended another level of education for me. Lucky me.

CHAPTER 7

THE ESTROGEN PATCH

The necessity of we "sentient writer types" to eventually share what we have learned from our solitary encounters with beauty. Writing and trying to figure out some stuff is such an important part of living.

From week sixteen, Jeffrey's Bay

Autopsy evidence, photographs and written reports of the laboratories and examiners were carefully prepared for presentation in court, even though some cases never went to court. The actual cause of death and surrounding circumstances were what trials were made of, and as in the States, sometimes it took years for a trial to be held.

A so-called AIDS case, the first of its kind in South Africa, had in 1996 reached the Supreme Court, a three-judge panel. Listening to the accused's testimony, the expert witness and the defense were riveting experiences for me. My mother had been a prosecuting attorney, and I had read, heard about and seen some of her trials, but never one like this. AIDS had not been an issue in those days, although lovers' quarrels ending in death had. With a wry smile she used to say that half of the murders were about sex and the other half about money. (And to the dismay of everyone in the police elevator, she once said to me "sometimes you can't tell the cops from the robbers.")

The victim in this Supreme Court case had been murdered by his good man-friend, who had been an affectionate and loyal comrade for years. While they had never had sex together he said, the accused, an attractive coloured man and a believable person to me, had openly admitted to some other homosexual

101

encounters. While to me he looked as though he might have been a gang member in his youth, he seemed like a regular citizen now. He did not have any tattoos that I could see, and he didn't have the "Cape Smile," or "flat smile," as it is known, which is produced by extraction of the top four front teeth, the incisors. The "flat smile" is, I was told, invariably a sign of gang membership and also had its uses in certain widely practiced homosexual acts.

The defendant said that his friend had been despondent about business and other things and had asked him one day to have sex together. They did. Afterwards, the friend had told the accused, a married man with children, that he was HIV positive and was sorry that he had gotten "carried away."

As his defense, the accused said that he had become so enraged at being betrayed and probably having been dealt a death blow that he had picked up a knife and stabbed his friend several times—to death. The Supreme Court eventually found him *not* guilty of murder, and not even guilty of assault.

As I recounted this story to both men and women there and in the U.S. I was surprised at how many people refuse to believe that supposedly good friends would consider having sex together, especially a married man with children. Others say it happens all of the time.

AIDS has been a much-denied and under-discussed subject on the huge multinational African continent until recently. But things have gotten so bad that even on television you see an articulate, handsome hunk of a guy demonstrating how to use condoms by holding a large wooden or plastic penis against his belly (low enough to be provocative and interesting to target audiences) and demonstrating the proper use. Probably useful information to those who see it, but many people only watch and listen to Christian stations, in Africa (and here), where information would never be disseminated in that way. "Condoms only promote promiscuousness," and "Prevent AIDS by being abstinent," are the sum and substance of the messages on these stations.

Yet all over southern Africa, as had been true throughout history, ragingly hormonal teenagers stare straight ahead and assiduously avoid touching each other in public, yet do all sorts of experimental things with each other in private. Some of them are the children of the righteous—pitiful tribute to sex education in the past and comprehension of the realities of the present. People are terrified of AIDS, but ignorance, carelessness and "tradition" often prevent even minimal protective action.

Still, there are knots of people, black and white, who say that the spread of AIDS is the fault of homosexuals who invaded Africa and that it is an intentionally designed plot. As for homosexuals coming from outside, the following article which was given to me by a German doctor in Namibia, is one of the most enlightening pieces I've read. It was in the "opposition" newspaper (meaning an Afrikaans view rather than the SWAPO government view) *The Namibian Weekender* in Windhoek, Namibia, on November 3, 1995.

ESKE KUUME
By Lazarus Jacobs

These people....
To say that I have always considered myself an African man is an understatement. I love this continent and all the customs, values and traditions that come with it. But one thing I have always hated about this beloved land is foreign domination.

That's why nobody could celebrate March 21, 1990 better than I did. It was out with the old and in with the new, I thought. But now to my dismay I hear some of our leaders saying that we still have an unwanted foreign import in our midst—homosexuals.

To begin with I ignored the news and controversy surrounding the topic, because I dismissed it as your usual "National Cha-Cha" madness. But as the insanity grew and as a concerned African I decided to acquaint myself with the subject. I asked a friend whether we had a word for "homosexual" in Oshiwambo. He quickly supplied the word *eshenge,* but warned me to be careful if I was going to write about "these people"—I might end up being called homophobic. Another big word, I thought.

The word *eshenge* started bothering me. Where does it come from? What does it mean? I asked myself. The problem begged for a call to my parents. First on the line was my father: "Hello Tate. What does *eshenge* mean?"

I waited in anticipation. After some hesitation and a short giggle of embarrassment Tate said: "He who is being approached from behind."

In his sudden silence I could hear my father praying that I wouldn't ask for an explanation. I must have waited a whole minute before I decided to ease the tension: "Did you also grow up with them or did they only appear in our generation?"

With a sigh of relief Tate replied: "They have always been around—since the beginning of time! These are people who were created by God and they should just be left alone!"

With this new information another question occurred to me: "How did you live with these people? Did you persecute them? Did you make fun of them? Just how did you share a village with them?"

Tate must have found my question funny, because he laughed before revealing: "No, they were given the right to do what they wanted. If they wanted to stamp *omanangu*, they were allowed to and if they wanted to herd cattle they could."

My father seemed pleased that he had fulfilled a paternal duty. Situations like this make me very proud of my background. The thing is my father is Kwanyama and my mother Ndonga.

When my mother came to the phone she was quick to say: "People like that are not known in my culture. The first time I saw any was when I went up north around Uukwanyama. You see, where I come from people like that would be given a good beating!" My mother sounded as if she had pronounced the final word on the subject. "But why Meme?" I protested.

Meme was too quick to respond: "People like that...are...they should be..."

I had never heard my mother struggling to answer me like that. I decided to help her out: "Isn't it because they were afraid of being beaten!"

After a sudden silence, Meme decided that Tate was better qualified to continue the conversation. Tate didn't hesitate to come to the phone and tell me: "If somebody says people like that were never part of us, laugh at them."

After performing our traditional how-are-yous I hung up and rushed to my computer.

When I ran the spellcheck on this article I was surprised to see the word "homophobic" highlighted, especially as "homosexual" was not. Perhaps our modern westernised society and the ancient traditions of Africa have something in common—a knowledge of homosexuality and a denial of the real problem.

There are "beware of AIDS and other sexually transmitted diseases" ads, articles, billboards and all manner of publicity, including posters announcing gay and lesbian festivals in major cities in South Africa and, to a lesser extent, in Namibia. But there is less of everything in Namibia except space, desert and animals.

A major museum in Pretoria was the site of a large and extremely graphic travelling AIDS exhibit in December. I was surprised when my host, a husband in a very up-scale suburb of Johannesburg, said that Pretoria was the gay capital of South Africa. The first thing most people said about Pretoria is that it is a very conservative community, but I guess nothing precluded both being true.

I was even more startled to learn that some few gay men in South Africa are completely giving up the gay life to live as heterosexuals and get married (to women.) I doubt that their numbers will significantly affect the ratio of straights to gays, but one formerly gay man that I know about is happily married, and by the time this manuscript is completed he will probably be a proud father.

The first television show I saw in South Africa, which originated in Johannesburg, was a lengthy, very musical and very humorous show with lots of female impersonators. At the end, a big point was made of interviewing some of the guys, who maintained that they were very heterosexual and happily married. A few of the wives were also interviewed and confirmed the stories. It's just that some men liked to dress up as women. And damn it all, some of those guys had gorgeous legs, to the dismay of us short-legged chunky people. But I also believe that throughout the world sometimes people find themselves trapped in a set of circumstances intolerable for them, including the person who says, "I am a woman in a man's body," or vice versa.

The longer I live the more I believe that just because some guy at some time ends up with another guy's penis in his hand, or two women end up in the same bed, does not make them a homosexual. I'm not sure what does, although every gay American man I have ever met has said that he had been that way since he was born, and the same for the few gay South African men I met who would talk about it. I am less certain about lesbian women, although I have heard the same "since birth" story from some.

I have three women friends in the States who have "lost their husbands" to men, and know four men whose wives have left them for women. (And I overheard a noisy conversation by two men about that subject in a fashionable watering hole in Cape Town.)

On several occasions I have heard both the men and the women say "You have no idea how bad it was living with him (or her)," with reasons ranging from violence or money to impotence or frigidity, habits or just plain lack of adequate affection. Sometimes it's a realization that he or she simply prefers same-sex relationships for what ever reason.

My guess is that most Americans, most white people and most of the Asians I know, don't touch other people or get as much real affection as they would like. And talk about feeling, admitting, and practicing real love of other people somehow is, well, just not done enough.

Overt affection and unapologetic love often seem very

natural among people with more pigment than I have. Most of us with lots of Anglo blood are not famous for displaying affection openly, and many people are reluctant to really hug or hold hands or be naked or ask about some body thing for fear of "living under suspicion" of being gay. The whole matter of touch is often badly handled, complicated and misunderstood, like the unwanted, clumsy or truly inappropriate touch. And saying "I love you" because you really do, can be a loaded proposition.

Although October was technically spring in Cape Town, a left-over winter storm rendered the city extremely cold and wet. I had on the expensive new hiking boots I had just bought, blue jeans, my deceased brother's tan cashmere V-neck sweater (a warm jersey, as it's known) over a black turtleneck tee shirt. And fortunately I had my London Fog raincoat to wear. The wind was piercing in those storms, and umbrellas got turned inside out. I walked into a restaurant for breakfast. Not finding a table, I asked a man at a table with extra chairs if I could join him— apparently something that South Africans will forgive in Americans, but rarely do themselves.

He was a tall, thin, awkward-looking young man with slick black hair severely parted on the right. He stood up, and with that wonderful British accent that everyone has, said, "Pleasure." It turned out he played the violin in the Cape Town Symphony and worked in a nearby bookstore during the day. So we talked about music and books, South Africa and "America" as South Africans almost invariably call the States.

Several days later the weather had warmed up a bit. I had on a tailored white L.L. Bean broadcloth shirt, the tan sweater draped over my shoulders, pale blue summer slacks, a buff colored belt and white sneakers, and, as always, my shoulder bag held tightly toward my front. I walked down the steep hill from my flat in Tamboerskloff as part of my "morning constitutional," decided to have breakfast out—and there he was again. He smiled, nodded, stood and gestured for me to sit down. We talked about books and music and Cape Town. He said he had a pass and invited me to the symphony that night, saying he would give me a ride if I lived near the restaurant, but that he couldn't give me a ride back because he had to visit a friend.

I definitely didn't mind going to things alone, especially

musical events. But the wonderful old City Hall, now Symphony Hall, is in a famously tough part of town. One taxi fare is better than two, so I accepted, drew a map on the "serviette" (paper napkin) showing him how to get to my flat, strode up to the counter to pay my bill and left.

That night as we silently waited to pull out of my driveway into the street, he said "Are you a lesbian?"

I was quite taken aback and after a minute of looking at him intensely said, "No, why do you ask?"

"You sort of dress that way, and you walk tough."

"Damn right I walk tough, and I don't plan to get mugged."

"I feel sorry for anyone who tries to mug you," he said.

"So do I," I said.

Not really paying attention to the traffic in the road as we rolled forward, he looked at me and timidly asked "You have had some experience? Yes?"

After a pause, I started to say "When I was eighteen I…" The screech of tires trying to stop and his stomp on his brake pedal avoided a terrible crash by inches. A car had been speeding down the hill as he pulled out without looking. Nervously he drove us to the symphony in total silence. That was the last I saw of him.

Deciding or defining and dealing with one's own sexuality takes a major effort and is often never fully resolved. I suddenly found myself in that position. At age sixty-six I had been forced by an event in South Africa to deal.

The forties and fifties were dreadful decades in my opinion. I was stuck with being a teenager during World War II, had a hideous, unproductive time in a Detroit public school as my parents' marriage disintegrated and my epileptic brother got sicker.

My parents were acrimoniously separated and divorced when I was fifteen, and it was on the front page of the newspapers because they were movers and shakers. The illusion was that because of the life-style we led (and the Ford connection) we had money; but my mother was nearly destitute, and so was my father. My brother was institutionalized, and I was stuck in a fashionable girls' school, constantly reminded of my parents' hatred of each other and in a cold part of the world that I disliked. Society and my family had a set of expectations not of my choosing all laid out for me. I was embarrassed, angry and puzzled about their divorce, my brother's epilepsy and why I was in this situation. Things seemed pretty bleak, but I graduated and could hardly wait to get away to college. What a relief that would be.

I got a summer job as a counselor in a camp in New England and—*pow.* I fell in love with a fascinating, beautiful fellow counselor, a girl—a person I could talk with, who cared for me, who didn't yell at me and made me feel very comfortable. And yet for reasons that I couldn't explain, I simultaneously felt very uneasy. Lots of clandestine hugs and kisses and looks. In hindsight, these were not really sexual, but I thought so at the time. Joy, confusion and guilt reigned.

Things were gravely compounded when I got home and a married woman friend of my family's seemed to sense my confusion. The most generous way I can put it now is to say she "moved in for the kill," ostensibly to try to comfort me during these difficult times."

The few weeks before I could get away to college were ghastly. Touch feels good, guilt feels bad, and in those days you didn't question the wisdom or actions of older people. I was so distressed that I made a secret appointment with a friend of the family who was a psychiatrist.

I guess nothing he could have said would have put me at ease. He said the camp thing was "normal"—I didn't believe him—and to get away from the older person. Hard to do, because she often came unannounced to our house, and as is often the case in these kind of exploitive situations, I was paralysed with fear, guilt and silence. I continued to write to my fellow camp counselor friend for a few months until the relationship just became too long distance and demanding, and everything but the memories faded away.

But bitterly and abruptly I terminated the other relationship with a luckily correct guess that the same sequence of events had happened to her when she was young. A nasty confrontation about staying out of my life followed. She died a few years ago, I suspect without ever resolving the matter of her own needs and preferences. And I now know that she drank too much, probably was an alcoholic, and that her generation never had a chance to sort things out. My anger was immense for a long time, but now I feel—for lack of a better word, forgiveness, if that is appropriate, and at least some understanding.

That summer in 1950 was enough to cast self-doubt, and for years was a gnawing problem that I had tried unsuccessfully to understand, accept or erase. But the uncertainties lingered.

Finally I left college as a geologist, and I now understand that being in a classically male profession didn't help matters in the eyes of some people. But I loved the beauty, the silence, the science and the chances to think and be alone. I certainly didn't want to be an elementary school teacher like so many of my female classmates, or immediately get married, live in a little apartment with squalling kids and have my worth measured by the size of my collection of Revere Ware pans and how shiny I kept the copper bottoms. These were the 1950s expectations for women of "my class."

My first job as a geologist was far from home and my past. I had a good number of serious men friends, happily lost my virginity and now have few regrets and more understanding of what I now know has happened to many women my age.

As a sexagenarian testatrix (an Arizona term meaning a woman in her sixties who has executed a will) and with the aid of my estrogen patches, I still think about sex a lot (as opposed to almost all of the time when I was younger). I continue to be a very physical person who thoroughly enjoys all of the many senses. I recognize that affection is, or should be, part of sex, but the obverse is certainly not necessarily true—a reality that confuses many people.

Thanks to a special kind of South African experience, I clearheadedly will continue to dress in L.L. Bean broadcloth shirts, wear my hiking boots when I feel like it, be willing to experiment, to risk (and sometimes lose), to walk tough, to be a hugging, touching physical person who drinks whiskey, swears and speaks her mind. Being compelled to face something and getting it right the second time around has been a great satisfaction.

CHAPTER 8

TRIBES

As I lock my balcony door, which I am told and know I must do at night, I see a slow moving middle-aged black woman walking down the hill on the other side of the street with a yellow plastic bag, skinny legs and black shoes, bulging brown coat that flares out like a tepee and a brilliant red turban. Her graceful swing is interrupted now and then with the side-step of a little stumble. Drunk? Drugs? Hungry? Desolate? That terrible desperation that I witnessed among black people when I was a child in Detroit is everywhere here. I feel so linked to every pain and every fog wisp and leaf movement. I am often preoccupied with how to have things be more equal, or at least fair.

From day one, week one, Cape Town

I am part of an ill-defined tribe that has no special name, no single place of origin, and few distinguishing customs. So what am I? More or less a white Anglo-Saxon Protestant with Scottish, English and Canadian ancestors. A lot of people who have similar backgrounds aren't anything like me. We don't act, look or think alike, and usually we would never meet, and probably wouldn't like each other if we did. Ultimately, I am known as an American. Not a very exact term, since Canadians, Mexicans and Central Americans are from the same continent and in that sense "American." Even the term North American doesn't quite cut it. Perhaps the specific appellation "American" came into being because United Statesian is a cumbersome term.

The current fad is to call someone Irish-American or Italian-American or Chinese-American. While I used to go along with

African-American, since I've spent time on the African continent, that barely works for me. In Africa you are not an African-African. In Africa, if you are a Zulu, you are a Zulu. If you are Herero, you are Herero. If you are a Xhosa, you are a Xhosa, if you are Ndebele, that's what you are—that's what you look like, that is your language, that is how you are known to yourself, your ancestors, your children and your friends and enemies. If you are a Tutsi or a Hutu you recently have been killing each other simply because that's what the two tribes have decided to do to each other.

Traditional values, customs, leadership methods and ownership systems are still the rule in many areas, including the independent countries of Lesotho and Swaziland, which are surrounded by the new South Africa. But the tribes, languages and ethnicity of their peoples overlap national boundaries.

The western civilizations have no monopoly on ruthless competition, jealousy, righteous indignation, greed, corruption and craziness. The worldwide legacy of these less-than-noble traits is the senseless undirected hatred, and sometimes the meticulously directed quest for vengeance. A lot of that is going on in southern Africa, but the incredible thing to me is the astonishing approach to reconciliation, the wide-spread attitude that "Okay, we may have done horrible things to each other, but it is in everyone's best interest that we work on what unites us rather than what separates us."

But still, the worldwide phenenomenon of the refugee isn't really being dealt with. I feel the problem is represented by the homeless in New York or Tucson, Africa or Bosnia and am distressed about what kind of world will soon be left when those "who roam about with no place to go and no place to call home" reach overwhelming numbers.

Until recently, and still in some places, it was a strong taboo to marry a person from another tribe, but I did meet a number of "mixed-tribe" persons in Africa. Some identities seem to be breaking down while others intensify. It's the same in the States. I have met Indians whose fathers were Cree and mothers Sioux; or Navajo and Gila, and many other combinations. Simultaneously there are efforts at establishing strong identity as a unit—Native American—while preserving the individual identities of Indian nations. Unfortunately, for us the States things are getting ugly as people claim a certain percent of Indian ancestry, because just the right percent makes one eligible for land or to share in the profits from reservation gambling— in my view, an ultimate curse for all concerned.

As the weeks passed I came to know more about history and the great variety of cultures and tribes in southern Africa. The history as we know it today, intimately linked with Namibia and other neighboring countries, is complex and fascinating, involving Dutch, British, German, Indian, Asian, mulatto and numerous distinct black tribes.

Nelson Mandela's autobiography presents a wonderful portrait of a simple childhood life as a member of one of the tribes of the Xhosa nation. Through a complexity of birth order, Mandela was selected to be educated and on the first day of school arbitrarily given the English name of Nelson, because, he says, "the whites were unable or unwilling to pronounce an African name." Although full of rich history, traditions, customs and taboos for over twenty generations, Xhosa was not viewed as a "culture" by the British.

Tribal identity matters, sometimes more than citizenship of the country in which you presently reside. When a person is asked for his name when away from his homeland, the reply can be several names. That happened to me in Namibia.

As I was working on my laptop one morning in the lobby of a hostel in the Namib Desert, the duties of two young waitresses were completed and they drifted over my way, obviously full of curiosity. I invited them to look over my shoulder and eventually to peck out their names on the keyboard. One did, and one didn't want to.

TJIUNOMUINJO-VICTORIN-KAZAPUA she typed quickly, complete with hyphens, using only two fingers but trying to mimic my whole-hand approach. I had her drill me on pronunciation of her name and then asked some questions. She said Tjiunomuinjo was her home name, the place that she and her family were from, and no matter where she was living, she used it as identification and a badge of honor. She was Herero, and Tjiunomuinjo was an area on the Skeleton Coast. Next was her given name and then her surname. She was twenty-one, and instantly I felt that she was a natural when it came to the use of computers. And so I stated, out of her hearing, to the manager of the hotel. To my delight he said that he had thought so too and was thinking about having her work at the front desk.

I reflect on the people all over the world who didn't get the right break at the right time. Such a waste of talent. The Mandela autobiography has a lot to say about fortuitous circumstance coupled with natural ability. But one person's apparent good fortune can be viewed as a loss to the tribe.

I have mixed feelings about "natives on display," no matter who or where. The reality is that people like me probably would only rarely get to be close to, talk with and really experience some customs without the contrivance of a tour.

The closest I came to really "living it" was during the three months that my family lived in Nome, Alaska, surrounded by Eskimos. We shopped at the same places, talked in the streets, shared many things including kids and toys. As a neighborhood youngster would walk out of our house with something that I had laboriously selected and packed for my own kids to play with, I was quickly reminded that it wasn't stealing or even just being a thoughtless kid. In that society, just about everything belongs to everyone, and it or some other toy would eventually drift back. It was at times disconcerting, but at times wonderful to be in a thief-free environment, to enjoy the smoked salmon and be able to say "No thank you, I don't care for any whale blubber." And to promise Bessie Moses I would try to find her son when I got back to San Francisco. He had been taken off an ice floe hunting seals and given a job by the Bureau of Indian Affairs—picking grapes in the hot summer in the Livermore Valley, California.

Earlier I mentioned my good fortune to have discovered the "cross-cultural" Tebu Tours in Pretoria. I had been several places with them and wanted to go see the bead workers and wonderfully adorned houses of the Ndebele. Three of us again were in Tebello's car, listening to his wonderful bass voice narrating details about that village or this township or that boondoggle public building in the middle of nowhere. We were headed for Kwandebele; the "Kwa" simply meant "place of," which clarified several other things for me, including KwaZulu Natal, the place where the Zulus live in the province of Natal.

There were several Ndebele villages far back off the road. We were traversing a dreary flat, gray, treeless scrub landscape when suddenly brilliantly painted symmetrical geometric designs painted on the walls of small thatch-roof houses punctured the dullness. Some of the designs looked like those on Navajo rugs, except that they were so colorful. Here and there flanking a doorway were symmetrically placed pairs of "barber poles" in bright blue, yellow and orange, meticulously detailed with black and white bars. We went to the most "developed" and touristy village, which apparently had a much better water supply, judging from the large trees and diminutive green pastures. There were a couple of small tourist vans, but we weren't herded around. Tebello knew everyone, and it was different being with a black man who spoke enough of their language to communicate. Extra things like good conversations with some of the bead workers were made possible for us.

One (an American one) might have said that the Ndebele were really far out. Everyone's head was shaved and bands of intricate bead-work were draped in certain ways to signify everything from wealth and marital status to things I knew nothing about. The women wore stiff, rectangular, elaborately beaded aprons, in addition to thick hoops of single-color beads resting on their shoulders or around their necks, wrists and ankles. Up to six inches of seamless, wide, gold-colored metal rings fit snugly around their ankles and necks...forever.

Another astonishing thing to me was that even on a sweating hot day, the middle-aged and older women wore identical thick, heavy blankets with four broad vertical bands of maroon, yellow, blue and red. As some of the women were engaged in relaxed conversation, the blanket would slip a little, revealing naked breasts. No big deal to anyone.

Sometimes the blankets were put over one shoulder and tucked around under an arm to leave a hand free to work. A grandmother with exceptionally beautiful headbands and a necklace of square beaded segments sat on a mat on the ground with her legs straight ahead covered by a square of white cloth. Many colors of tiny beads filled an indentation in the cloth between her knees, and one by one she picked up beads on the tip of a needle and sewed them into the picture or design in her mind. I was struck that relatives of friends of mine look and act just the same when they do quilting. Exchange this woman with a quilter from Philadelphia and they would do wonderfully. I kept asking myself, why must people hate and fear each other, when we are so much alike?

One of my first nights after my first arrival in Cape Town I wrote in my laptop notes:

> Three in the morning I wake up cold. The trees whip and the wind slants the winter-like rains of spring with the cold of the soul of deepest winter. Where is my lady with the red turban who sleeps under my window?"

Her costume changed as we went from formal spring into formal summer. Her gate changed and her sleeping ground sometimes changed from a few blocks away to the oleander bushes right under my window. I saw her emerging from the bushes on my very early-morning walks. She had become a symbol for me.

Sometimes she and a man or several other people would be there buried in the white oleander blossoms, undetectable except for someone's occasional cough. Sometimes terrible smells would rise up the half story to my balcony. Sometimes she would be terribly drunk and rambling down the street wailing as the man tried to quiet her. Often in the morning there would be trash under the oleanders, but I would have heard nothing and the people had disappeared. Sometimes I would encounter her or other people picking through the apartment's half-dozen plastic trash barrels looking for papers or plastic or cardboard or cans to sell. I felt especially disrupted when I would pass by and she would be eating something without looking up.

I reluctantly mentioned the sequence to my landlord when I had lost parts of three nights sleep in a row. His face tightened. Apparently it had been going on for months, if not years. They used to sleep under *his* oleanders, but he took to throwing buckets of water out his window which caused them to move on.

She came from somewhere before she ended up under my

bushes. She probably knows what tribe she springs from, at least I hope so, to provide her some scrap of identity. Chances are she drifted into the metropolitan area from one of the numerous peripheral shanty towns. The disparities of our fortunes—hers and mine—were so uncomfortable for me that I could not bring myself to stop her, to talk with her...about what?, to give her money or clothes or food. To be Miss Curious Busy Body seeking information to broaden my understanding or maybe to research an article?

Her life never could have been reasonable because poverty and apartheid had been in existence for many years longer than its formal "creation" by the so-called architect of apartheid, Dr. Hendrik Verwoerd, around 1950. She had never known anything else and was now too broken to grasp many of the changes.

Structured, intentional poverty has destroyed much that has been beneficial to mankind since the beginning. When people are hungry, they will steal. When they have nothing they also have nothing to lose by attempting to acquire, except their lives. And that's not such a big deal to many; actually it would be a relief.

I already knew that what was happening to my lady in the red turban was unfair; and her being a woman didn't help matters, because women are second or essentially nothing of importance in some tribes (including some tribes of white males!). But the new Constitution of South Africa changes those legalities, at least on paper. The piece of paper, with enforcement behind it, gradually helped to change attitudes.

Unlike our Constitution, which took years to acknowledge the rights of half the population (women), the South African Constitution embraces just about all that Americans now say they care about. I like to think that they learned some things from us. Some good things.

I visited the sister of a friend in Okahandja, Namibia, a small town north of Windhoek. The town was laden with history but not many monuments. Every year the Herero tribe had an important gathering there. Okahandja also was famous for the vegetables raised by a Portuguese farmer, and for its native wood carvers. At each end of town along the side of the road was a block-long string of beautiful wood carvings of animals, art objects and lovely furniture. Shacks behind the displays provided the housing for the carvers, although there were other villages along the road to Windhoek.

As mentioned elsewhere, Namibia is a sparsely populated and much more tranquil country than South Africa, although the two have many similarities, including squatter villages that are very segregated. One tribe each. There is very little mixing, and tribal custom often perpetuates the exclusivity. Tribal rivalries and distrust have a long history and the ways are not very understandable to the casual visitor. German-like authoritarianism still prevails in many situations, and of course there are police and soldiers and courts; but tribal ways handle many circumstances.

As we drove into town there was a sizable knot of black people facing away from the road back by the clothes-lines, smoldering fires and small houses made of just about anything. The next day when we drove out to see the nearly empty dam, the crowd was still in more or less the same position. When I noticed the same gathering the next day I asked my hostess about it.

There had been three murders of this tribe's members in recent weeks. Three days ago they had sent a person to a neighboring camp to inquire and he had not returned. My hostess said that this was a meeting to decide who was best prepared to find out the truth and go next to try to stop the killing. She said the meetings sometimes lasted three days and then dissolved; they didn't break up until there was consensus. There would be an action, and the police would not be involved (in part, she said because many officers wouldn't dare enter the camp except heavily armed and in large numbers). But many officers didn't really care too much about "a few dead Indians," as people used to say in the U.S. And nobody would reveal anything to the police anyhow.

In several senses the Boers could be called a tribe. They wanted (many still want) to be racially "pure" and live in their own white homeland, which has shaped a great deal of their history. These decendents of the original Dutch and French settlers in Southern Africa do have a special look. They are big and blocky, and while some are light of foot, they strike the casual observer as, shall we say, plodding. In a fascinating book by Stephen Kanfer about the De Beers empire he says, descriptively, that no Boer woman over thirty years of age weighs less than 180 pounds.

In black southern Africa, tribes squabbled viciously among themselves, with the Zulu often coming out on top. But often there were internal struggles as well; a famous Zulu chief was murdered by his brother in a power struggle. But policies of conquest and brutality toward neighboring tribes continued, and Zulu warriors ensured for themselves a prominent place in history that persists to this day.

In the first quarter of the 1800s the British rulers of South Africa instituted what were called "pass laws," some of the earliest roots of institutionalized racism and apartheid. Blacks had to have permanent addresses, and since they couldn't own property they were under the control of some white person and couldn't "pass" from one place to another without the permission of that person—a regulation that was fine in the eyes of most white people. Eventually, however, liberals in Britain were so outraged that the pass laws were repealed, which outraged most South Africans, including the Boers.

The Boers, leaving more than fleeing the hated British, started trekking right into Zulu territory. The Zulus took advantage at every turn, raiding wagon after wagon, murdering men, women and children, even inviting the Boers to sit down to discuss peace and then cracking their skulls with the famous knobkerries. Until one night when Andreis Pretorius said (I paraphrase), "circle the wagons, boys and girls. God is on our side, and if he lets us win this one, we vow to do something to honor him." They had artillery and elephant guns.

Children loaded guns, women shot and were shot, as were men. Despite the hoardes—thousands and thousands—of Zulu, it was guns versus short spears. So many Zulus were killed that the Ncome River ran red and was renamed and still is called the Blood River. The vow, the covenant made with God on that December 16, was honored, and the church of the covenant was built in Pietermaritsburg.

That battle was a scene reminiscent of many in the American West, and thanks to a plethora of movies about the

American West, most Americans think they invented the circling of wagons. To use Stefan Kanfer's analogy to a play: "In Act One the white invaders are driven back by local tribes; in Act Two the foreigners' technology brings them victory after victory until the final surrender. This is interpreted as a sign of divine approval. Act Three shows 'native policy' put in place by the new rulers."

I was reminded of stories that my father used to tell me about the Rouge (red) River that runs through the Henry Ford estate, Fair Lane. Detroit was founded in 1702 by the French, and hence there are lots of French names. The naming of the Rouge was based on a similar incident, the killing of enough Indians to make it run blood red.

Most of the world's religions teach some kind of love and don't overtly advocate killing, although there are a lot of blood-thirsty passages and calls for vengeance in the Bible. As crimes become more abundant and brutal in the States, revenge has been on the increase. None of this "turn the other cheek" stuff, just "turn her/him over to me for a minute" blood lust. In the old days, in both America and Africa, the prevailing and often stated view of many was that "the only good red man/black man is a dead one."

The African National Congress has been protesting the plight of disenfranchised black people of Southern Africa since its founding in 1913.

CHAPTER 9

T-SHIRTS AND MUSIC

The study of a nation's arts makes a significant contribution to its cultural maturity and well-being, and consequently to improved social and personal relations.

Andrew Tracey, Director
International Library of African Music

Knowing that it was my intent to somehow become involved in the jazz and blues scene in Africa, the Director of the Tucson Jazz Society jammed half a dozen music related T-shirts and a couple of CDs into my already stressed luggage. Earlier I had packed about a dozen T-shirts from the Tucson Poetry Festival, and others from the Tucson Blues Society, the Tucson Symphony, and WorldTeach, a Harvard literacy program that has branches in South Africa and Namibia and with which I had been affiliated for a year in Ecuador.

Since its inception fifteen years ago, the Tucson Poetry Festival, an annual three-day event, has become a world-class gathering of major poets and other artists from everywhere. Each year a good looking T-shirt is created, with the list of participants on the back. I had a splendid collection...all but two. It was time to share them.

After spending October in my leased Cape Town flat at the foot of Table Mountain, I took the immaculate two-decker Captour Mainliner bus for an eighteen-hour trip to Windhoek, the capital of Namibia. From a comfortable seat on the top deck, through spotless windows I could see my beloved Table Mountain and the sparkling harbor receding as we drove north.

We glided through the incredibly beautiful wine country near Stellenbosch. Miles of tidy green vineyards in long perfect lines on perfectly tilled earth led up to the spectacular surrounding mountains. Then we turned north through empty bushy green areas called *fynbos,* which had just ended their spectacular show of the many unusual spring wildflowers of South Africa. (Sadly, months later much of that country would be burned blank by raging wildfires.)

As we imperceptibly rose toward the large, rolling fields of newly planted corn and wheat, one of the neatly uniformed hostesses served cups of Coke or Fanta. Fortunately no one was sitting next to me so I could stretch out my Ace-bandaged leg, broken years ago but always needing to be elevated a few times a day. I had been advised by friends to get out and stretch at each stop, which I did. That's when you meet and get to talk with the smokers and other people.

The hostess came by with soft drinks again and presented a menu and asked if I wanted to order supper or simply get something at one of the rest stops that occurred every couple of hours. Usually I eat lightly when travelling, so I said no.

The messy ribs and bulging hamburgers that appeared later made me glad to stick to the canned juice, fruit and *Kudu biltong* I had brought with me. At the next fueling stop, I bought some Simba vinegar and salt potato chips and some banana-flavored milk, which sounded better than bubble gum flavored-milk, and settled in for the night.

The buses were luxurious, far superior to the Greyhound buses I had written a couple of articles about years earlier. On a strategically placed monitor I saw my first Bruce Lee movie and then *Philadelphia.* Some American movies had been smuggled in during the apartheid years, but nothing political or, God forbid, about AIDS would have been shown publicly until recently. *Cry the Beloved Country* was just opening for the first time in Cape Town.

As we headed north toward the equator, the temperature became noticeably warmer. I took off my vest and then my sweater, revealing the back of my poetry festival T-shirt to the woman in the seat behind me. At the next stop she asked me about it, and at each stop asked me more about it and why I was going to Namibia. Her name was Gertrude.

Except for seeing so many brilliant stars crowding each other in a velvet, black moonless sky, crossing the national border in the middle of the warm night was a long and dreary experience. The sky shed an eerie but lovely light over a barren, sandy scrub-bush terrain as our slow but orderly queue left the dirt path, entered a shabby little shack with bare light bulbs hanging down and showed an assortment of passports and papers to bored, partially uniformed immigration officials. The officials, clearly underpaid petty bureaucrats, sat behind a tall counter and pounded on the documents with old rubber stamps.

As I exited the shack, Gertrude, who was in front of me in the line, turned and announced loudly that she was a photographer for a paper in Windhoek and insisted that I must be interviewed because she surmised from the T-shirt that I was some sort of writer. With some embarrassment I said I would think about it. (It later happened.)

I wore a different T-shirt each day, and almost every day someone commented on it. I then asked, usually to their surprise, "Do you write poetry?" Almost invariably the startled answer was "Why, yes. How did you know?" I know, because all kinds of people everywhere in the world write poetry, although most never acknowledge it. So I said, "Just keep doing it," which invariably led to a smile and often to more conversation.

I was glad to find that there were lots of bookstores (with lots of poetry books) in both Namibia and South Africa. As elsewhere in the world, poetry readings were often well attended.

Later, at a lodge I stayed at in northern Namibia, the chef always stood by the breakfast table to greet and assist the visitors. He asked about my shirt, because, he said, he wrote a little poetry himself. I brought the shirt back to him as a gift after breakfast. A thrill for both of us.

In Pretoria I would take an evening stroll for the exercise and to watch the sun set and then get a snack at the gas station convenience store near my lodgings. The clerk admired my shirt and asked me if I would read some of his poetry. I was really touched that he would ask, so I did, and was very impressed by that young man's loves and hopes and aspirations. The day I left

I gave him a T-shirt and told him to keep doing it. He said he would.

Knowing that South Africa was big on the sport of rowing, I took a Detroit Boat Club sesquicentennial commemorative T-shirt—1839-1989. As a young man my father had been a coxswain and joined the Detroit Boat Club, now the oldest rowing club in the United States. The Boat Club had always been part of my life, and I knew each of the Filipino waiters by name. When you are little you don't think about such things as where did they come from and where do they live. We just knew we liked each other. It wasn't until years later that I learned that they all lived in a dormitory, had families back in the Philippines, didn't make very much money but were treated fairly well and had been specially recruited to work in this fancy white men's club. Certainly they were better off than the black men who were recruited to work in the gold mines of South Africa, but still they weren't really "free."

For a few days I stayed with the family of a geologist friend in a tony suburb of Johannesburg. One of the three boys was a poet, one followed in the footsteps of his father as an all-around-athlete—cricket, rowing and all that. In my Boat Club T-shirt I stood on the bank of a gigantic many-acre lake that now occupied an old gold mine as members of the King Edward VII rowing club raced against another club in eight-man shells circling the lake eight times. Nostalgia time for me. Their other son, a teenager, stayed home and watched a Mortal Kombat video while listening to Metallica. My sense is that he is vulnerable to what is beginning to happen on the drug scene.

There was just too much to do all of the time. I had hoped to visit several jazz clubs in Johannesburg, especially one that starred the brother of a cellist in the Cape Town Symphony. Aside from playing the cello he also was a terrific jazz musician. Like a lot of musicians the world over, he had to hold another job to make ends meet. He was a bartender in one of my favorite restaurants, and we just got talking. It began to seem curious to me how my encounters all seemed to lead in the same directions.

The longer one is in South Africa, the more an acute sense of the diversity of various parts of the country develops. Over and above differences, however, Africans are united by the love and use of music. No matter how joyous or how angry a demonstration may be, for example, someone starts singing or dancing (usually both) and everyone picks up the beat. Something very special happens.

There is much wonderful African music of all kinds, but more and more of the popular music sounds like touring groups from the rest of the world. A pamphlet called "African Music—An Endangered Heritage," published by the International Library of African Music, ILAM, says:

> The music taught in most African schools and black homeland universities owes little to Africa.
>
> The growth and direction taken by popular music in South Africa is very largely in the hands of the record industry. There has recently been a worldwide resurgence of interest in South African indigenous popular music, yet the music recorded and broadcast on most South African radio and TV stations retains a heavy emphasis on overseas commercial music....

Andrew Tracey, following in the footsteps of his father, Hugh, is working diligently and quite successfully to preserve and promote the incredibly rich African heritage. That same article continues, "South Africa, probably alone among countries of its stature, still has no published collection of its indigenous folk music. Most blacks know little about their own traditional music, let alone that of other groups in South Africa or the rest of Africa."

ILAM is a wonderful and fortunate thing for the world. The library is at Rhodes University in Grahamstown. That I visit there had been suggested to me several times before I left the States because it is a famous literary, cultural and musical center, among other things. (Dave Brubeck's son Darius even ended up there.)

So I called Tracey, the director, and was most graciously welcomed. I was invited to luncheon with his family, and visited the small factory where various African instruments are made of native woods by native people.

Whether in homes as musical instruments, as pieces of furniture or as art objects, I kept running into stinkwood, a dark, very dense, heavy and beautiful native wood that is becoming more and more expensive as the supplies diminish frighteningly fast. Several typically African types and sizes of xylophone were made in this small factory, and the richest, most resonant tones came from those made of stinkwood.

Tracey, a veritable pixie of a man, had an incredible collection of instruments at his office on the Rhodes University campus, where ILAM is housed. He can play every one and delights in doing so. He would thump rhythmically on a stinkwood xylophone or marimba and then on a pine one, just to show me the difference, and then he would pick up a pennywhistle or a small gourd with one string drawn taut over a small hole and begin to play and sing. There are lots of one-note instruments in Africa, and they use many different scales and tunings.

In a large, dark, air-conditioned room at ILAM, the walls were filled floor to ceiling with records, cassettes, and reel-to-reel tapes of African music, some of which had already vanished from the villages and countrysides where it used to be played or sung. Many decades ago Tracey's father had begun recording.

The librarian, a very smart and very tribal young woman, had just returned from the Smithsonian and our Library of Congress, where she had gone to learn more about preservation techniques. Severe problems were beginning to appear as the decades-old materials, like recording tape, began to disintegrate.

Churches are almost always a source of listening music (sometimes wonderful, sometimes not so) and cathedrals can afford to and have the talent to do the big stuff, like masses, requia and oratorios. The Anglicans are more or less the equivalent of Episcopalians in South Africa, and St. George's Anglican Cathedral in Cape Town is no exception in its music menu. The Faure requiem had always been one of the most important pieces of music to me. But at St. George's I got a double whammy: Faure and Desmond Tutu. He just happened to be preaching on that day, so I went up to talk with him afterwards. He was such an awesome figure that I was startled to see that he was probably not more than five-foot-five. When so many of the black, Indian and coloured leaders were banned, killed, exiled or imprisoned, it had been Tutu at that very church who kept the world aware of some of what was going on with apartheid.

As I have mentioned several times, coincidence, luck, fate, syncronicity or whatever you want to call it plays a big role in my life, never more so than during my time in southern Africa. I had brought Tom Ervin's trombone CD and a Jazzberry Jam Dixieland tape. I thought that as long as I was personally committed to doing what I could to get Sam Taylor a chance to play in South Africa, I might as well do the same for Jazzberry Jam and Tom. I had no authority except as friend and fan, and everyone understood that. It's all wonderful world-class music, and I wanted to share it with the world.

I had loaned the recordings to FMR, the Cape Town jazz and classics station, which, recognizing the quality of the music, had played several tracks that very day. The Ervin disc was sitting on Damon Durant's desk waiting for me to pick it up when the first trombone in the Cape Town Symphony walked by on his way to do a show for the station, and asked to borrow it. Of course, I said yes, and this acquaintance ultimately led me to Michael Blake.

Blake is the first trumpet in the Cape Town Symphony and founder of the Genesis Project, which teaches black kids in the townships to play traditional western brass instruments—an incredible source of talent for future classical and jazz music.

But Blake has carried it one step further. He also founded the well-known Solid Brass Quintet composed of members of the Cape Town Symphony, which plays classical and jazz music all over the country. Amapondo, a famous African percussion and marimba band considered by many to be "the guardians of African music" has numerous recordings and concerts around the world to their name. The brass quintet and members of Amapondo have been successfully merged in a unique and increasingly well-known group called Intsholo, a Xhosa word meaning sweet sounds. They were invited to play at the Olympics in Atlanta.

I have no illusions about how nasty people can be toward

each other, but it's things like Intsholo that make me so optimistic about the future of South Africa. Music crosses lines like nothing else.

One of the first things I observed when I wandered into the Longkloof Studios and found radio station FMR was an incredible series of photographic portraits by Rashid Lombard of African jazz greats lining the walls. The pictures had been comissioned by the Guinness Brewery for its 1995 calendar. I stopped and stared at the picture of Donald Tshomela, subconsciously squeezing my ears to listen closely in hopes of hearing him sing. It's that wonderful a picture. When I learned that Tshomela was also a boxer, I couldn't help but be reminded of Sam Taylor, who was also a championship boxer. Every picture in the calendar captured the feeling of the instrument as well as the artist, and, happily, it was my understanding that Lombard would also do the 1997 Guinness Jazz Greats calendar.

As in the U.S., liquor companies sponsor many sporting and musical events. Each year in mid-winter (July) Smirnoff vodka sponsors the jazz part of a huge music and arts festival in Grahamstown. I wished that Sam Taylor could get to Africa. I didn't know how, but I realized that he would get himself there if people heard his music. So I took his recordings to the radio station and to several clubs and musicians. I stayed for lunch at Mannenberg's Jazz Cafe, and an hour after I gave them the CD Sam Taylor became "music to have luncheon by." Actually it's better after lunch because there is so much intricacy to listen to.

Parts of South Africa are very hip. Cellular phones are on the ears of all young good-looking professional types as they walk around any downtown. BMWs and Mercedes abound and the number of yacht basins and "yachties" and people black and white with lots of discretionary capital multiply. There are Internet cafes, and CompuServe and other on-line services are available, although they were not usually working too smoothly while I was there. (I am told that they have improved greatly since I left. I now read a Johannesburg paper on the Internet almost every day. A note of miscellany: The small, high-density computer disks which we call little floppies are called "stiffies."

The numbers of typical real estate agents multiply, and a few are making millions. The likes of Michael Jackson, movie stars and world-famous personalities (including Maggie Thatcher's son) are looking at personal residential property. The Cape-to-Rio sailing races become more international and fashionable. Already there are micro breweries and a taste for single-malt scotches and flavored vodkas. Always there have been incredible wines, and wine is now an increasingly important export. (When Napoleon was in exile, reportedly he only wanted French champagne and South African port to drink.)

One of the most prominent spots on the wonderfully developed waterfront of Cape Town was the Green Dolphin, a restaurant which features jazz "eight nights a week." I struck up friendships with some of the owners, managers and waiters, talked about Sam Taylor and gave them a CD and a tape. One of the owners had just returned from Los Angeles, where he had heard Sam at B.B. King's. So I unloaded a couple of Jazz Society T-shirts and made arrangements to meet with an attorney and part-owner of the Green Dolphin, who also ran the Square Deals booking agency. The agency said they had a limited budget but wanted to invite Sam and Heather Hardy (the incredible blues violinist with Sam's band) to the Grahamstown Festival and would be in touch with his agent.

Much of the business end of music is very political, and full of rivalries and deals, as I found out (again) as I went from musical event to musical event. It was evident when I talked with the management of Mannenberg's Jazz Cafe and the dozens of others in the Cape Town area who wanted nothing to do with the Green Dolphin. It wasn't until later that I heard that Smirnoff had really pulled the rug on the budget, so nothing happened about getting Sam to Grahamstown (that year).

For the second year in a row, a loudly touted Cape Town Jazz Festival sponsored by Spencer-Miller Jazz Promotions landed on the rocks a few days before it was to begin. The '96 lineup was Diane Schurr, Maynard Ferguson, Earl Klugh, Tania Marie, the Count Basie Orchestra and Randy Crawford. I never did find out what happened, but with co-sponsors like KLM and American Express Travel Service it must have been something unusual.

During the apartheid years, famous musicians chose not to visit South Africa or their countries forbade them to do so. But the flood is on now, everyone from Kinky Friedman to Pavarotti. People with incredibly expensive tickets oohed and aahed at Pavarotti in a beautiful vineyard setting. Reviews were terrific, except for one, which in my view, told the truth.

Four months before Tina Turner was to appear, the cigarette king Peter Stuyvesant paid huge amounts for radio and print advertizing for Tina. Why? The answer had to be to promote the smokes, since Tina could fill any venue on two days' notice. It is sad to note how many young people are taking up smoking, and in addition to Marlboros, I was surprised at how popular Chesterfields were.

Different entrepreneurs bring in many groups, including the Cranberries and Crosby, Stills and Nash and others. There are numerous radio stations in most major cities, and even before the artists arrive, one has heard everything that they have ever recorded. This goes on about twice a day until they leave. Overkill, as far as I was concerned.

So, my T-shirts paid off wonderfully, and I had disposed of almost all of them. I know Damon was puzzled when I burst out laughing as he gave me a little going away present—an FMR T-shirt.

CHAPTER 10

NAMIBIA

I wakened early, not sure if I was hot or cold, a view of infinity out the window. You don't see wind here. But you hear it. God, you hear it. Nothing to move unless there is dirt. Red silt has already made a pattern on the broad entry course of ceramic tile.

From week seven, The Namib

Something happens to people when they visit the Namib, the world's oldest desert. The phrase "world's oldest" has no special meaning when you are there. It's hard to explain. As a matter of fact, it can't be explained. "What can you say?" is the only response when you meet someone who has been there. There are no words. You simply nod in unspoken understanding. Most people gasp in awe, or at least say "wow" when they see pictures of the Namib; but actual memories become burned into your soul.

On one of my first days in the capital of Namibia, Windhoek (pronounced VENT-hook), I found a postcard in a bookstore: an overwhelming picture of huge, dark sand dunes. I stood staring at it for I don't know how long. I took it to the clerk and said "Is this real?" She looked at me intently, slowly nodded her head and shrugged a yes.

I saw books and more cards. I could hardly believe the colors or the shapes: soft bald grace of tremendous proportions. There were angles, curves, slopes, contours, colors and motions that one never sees in so-called real life. The purity, the sizes and magnitudes of the dunes render even the most vocal person speechless. Changes in light and form are too swift for painters.

131

Photographers are the only ones with a chance.

On a map, Namibia looks like a dipper (a coincidence not lost on the water conservation authorities who use it in billboards to show present supplies of water, often frighteningly low.) The Caprivi, a skinny strip of land on the north leading east, is the handle.

Namibia was a German colony (German South West Africa) until the end of World War I, when South Africa was designated by the *League* of Nations to administer it as what was known as a mandated territory. Not only did the Germans "own" South West Africa, they also controlled German East Africa, which is now Tanzania. The Caprivi strip was to be part of a corridor linking the two colonies along the Zambezi River.

Germany was a latecomer in the colonization game but made up time with traditional efficiency, and in the case of the five or so major tribal groups of black people they found in South West, outdid themselves in their "whites are superior to blacks" attitude in incredibly cruel ways.

Captured documents indicated the policies and opinions that were universally abhorred in World War II were earlier refined by the Germans in South West Africa, including by the notorious Herman Goering's father. What always amazes me is how the Germans kept such perfect documentation, including records that tell you what they are going to do (*Mein Kampf*) that they're doing it, and then tell you how they did it.

The Union of South Africa was given control of German South West Africa after World War I. While the white South Africans of that period were every bit as racist and greedy as the Germans, they weren't as open about it and turned out to be consummate liars. And on top of that they were cattle thieves—the ultimate indignity for the herdsmen, especially Hereros, whose wealth was measured in cattle.

Hereros were viewed as the most sophisticated of the Namibian tribes, and while they themselves engaged in a number of brutal and warlike activities, including conquering their neighbors and making slaves of the Berg-Damaras, their leaders had the sense to know that they needed to be governed, or at least assisted, by whites in the changing technological world in which they found themselves. They didn't know how to drill bore holes for water and didn't have vehicles or the equipment and technology of the white man.

Many African tribes had hideous experiences with the British, but the Brits were generally viewed by the natives as more honorable than the Germans or the South Africans about keeping promises and paying debts. So when the United Nations came into existence after World War II, the Hereros petitioned to become a British protectorate, a ward of the U.N. or a protectorate of the United States; but they did *not* want to be under the South Africans. It became clear that the South Africans were willing to kill the chiefs to keep power and to be able to claim land more easily. The principal chief of the Hereros fled to Bechuanaland (now Botswana), because as long as he was alive, the tribe still owned the land.

A parallel exists during our own Salem witch trials, when an accused would have heavy stones piled on his chest until he confessed his sin of being a witch. If he confessed to witchcraft, his relatives couldn't inherit his land. In a famous case, Giles Corey kept saying "more weight" as they piled on stones until his chest was crushed and he died. But his wife and kids *did* get his property.

The South Africans ostensibly conducted all sorts of surveys that indicated that the Namibian tribes wanted to be ruled by South Africa. The South Africans altered documents, destroyed others and self-righteously presented to the U.N. the "wishes" of the tribes to be governed by them. Not so.

The mandate status that had been developed for various countries by the League of Nations had been replaced with the trusteeship status created by the United Nations. After much squabbling, South Africa was permitted to keep "ruling" Namibia, but under the terms of the original mandate—which they had for so long interpreted in accordance with their own views, not with the well-being of the natives as required by the mandate rules.

When I first arrived in Windhoek one of the first street signs I saw read "Michael Scott Boulevard." Fascinated, I asked several people, "Who is Michael Scott?" Not one person had the foggiest idea. But I knew; and never had I anticipated that another piece of my past would rise up to be "re-grasped" in such a place.

Living in Detroit, Michigan in the immediate post-World War II era didn't ensure that one knew anything about black people or got along with them, but opportunities existed. As an assistant prosecuting attorney, my mother had ample contact with black judges, police, detectives, politicians and criminals. She was appointed a special delegate to the three-year-old United Nations, and it wasn't until much later, when I was reviewing her papers, that Michael Scott and what he had meant to do became clear to me.

Betsy Graves Reyneau, a family friend, did a series of portraits of famous American negroes that toured the United States in the late 1940s. I—in my early teens—liked Betsy and I liked her paintings. Vaguely I understood that the show had something to do with raising money for a preacher named Michael Scott, who was coming to the fledgling United Nations to get them to do something, I wasn't sure what, about some black people in Africa.

The Hereros and other tribes had asked an intense, dedicated and intelligent, but by his own account somewhat scruffy, Anglican minister, who had earlier been kicked out of South Africa, to go to the United Nations meetings and truthfully represent their interests, which South Africa was not doing. Just the mechanics of getting from Africa to the meetings at Lake Success, New York, in 1947 and later to meetings in Paris were daunting, especially with little money and a vilifying press in several countries. Scott was labeled a troublemaker, a ne'er-do-well, non-credentialed, and so on. Every epithet imaginable was flung at him and his purpose. But gradually the contrasts of positions on governing the tribes in Namibia were clearly drawn—black and white, one could say.

One of the results of the Michael Scott intrusion into the U.N. was to alter the organization in a critical and unanticipated way. As Freda Troup puts it, there was "…The recognition of the right of unrepresented minorities to appeal past their governments to world opinion." Scott was very touched by part of a prayer of former Herero chief Hosea Kutako: "O Lord, help us who roam about. Help us who have been placed in Africa and have no dwelling place of our own...." The problem of "bulk refugee status" continues to this day in several places in the world, including the Balkan states.

Strict observation by the U.N. and others of the South African practices in the mandated territory continued until 1989, when things became so bad that Namibia was declared to be administered jointly with the United Nations, which it was until it became independent shortly thereafter.

Most of the northern boundary of Namibia is shared with the troubled country of Angola. During the recent long altercations involving communist Cuban troops, the largely conservative and communist-hating South African Defense Forces were quietly but immensely active in Namibia, especially in the north.

Much violence occurred during the long-fought wars along that border. There were many under-discussed aspects, like the counterinsurgency Koevoet (pronounced KOO-foot) which was mainly black Africans fighting beside the South African army and Defense Forces (apparently in great racial harmony) against SWAPO, the South West Africa People's Organization. SWAPO was backed by the Americans and the United Nations and became the prevailing party, but there were violent atrocities on all sides.

After the victory of the SWAPO movement, Namibia became an independent one party democracy in 1990 and remains so as of this writing—which is not to say that there isn't opposition, including opposition press.

The bush war along the Angola/Namibia border that brought SWAPO to power was complex and is still extremely controversial. The points of view seem cast in concrete in the minds of those who will talk about it. Except for vaguely understood news accounts in the '80s that used the word SWAPO, which somehow was linked to the "mess with those communists and Cubans in Angola," most westerners, and for that matter some Africans, didn't know what was going on there, and still don't.

The subject was first brought to my attention while I was visiting white English/Afrikaans-speaking Namibian friends in Okahandja. I was shown a book called *Koevoet! The Inside Story*, by

American journalist Jim Hooper. The jacket said that he was "the first journalist ever granted unrestricted access to…the notorious South West African Police Counterinsurgency Unit known as Koevoet." The slick, 240-page book had an ISBN, lots of black-and-white and some colored pictures, was published by Southern Book Publishers in Johannesburg, copyrighted by Hooper in 1988 and was dedicated to his family. The copy I saw had a sticker saying CNA, a big chain bookstore in southern Africa. I was told that I must read the book to understand Namibia and South Africa. I read a bit at my friend's home in Okahandja but then had to leave. In Windhoek I couldn't find a copy at any bookstore, and then I remembered that I had been told that it probably would be hard to find, maybe impossible. So, with a very full schedule ahead, I dropped the matter until later.

When I got back to South Africa I couldn't find a copy of *Koevoet!*, not even at the same chain book store (CNA) at which my friend's copy had been purchased. Some book dealers professed not to know the title or to have only vaguely heard of it. The South African families I stayed with, with the exception of one, didn't seem to know what I was talking about when I mentioned *Koevoet!* When I got back to the States, I couldn't find a copy and booksellers would only say that it was out of print.

Out of the blue, some South African friends loaned me a copy and said it was a book I must read to understand South Africa and Namibia. A librarian found one copy of *Koevoet!* in the Library of Congress and said that there was also a book called *Beneath the Visiting Moon—Images of Combat in Southern Africa* by Jim Hooper. I asked her to get the latter for me. It was a slick, 264-page book, had lots of pictures, and an ISBN, was dedicated to B.J.B. and to H.R., was published and copyrighted in 1990 by Lexington Books (D.C. Heath and Company, Lexington, Massachusetts and Toronto) as part of Lexington's series on Issues in Low-Intensity Conflict. There is a copy of *Beneath the Visiting Moon* in my local library, which I read, and nowhere did I find a reference to the book *Koevoet!* It's the *same* book with very minor changes—like the dedication.

My librarian friend said that there was no legal requirement to reference one book to the other, for example on a page saying "other books by this author." But my difficulty in obtaining a copy could certainly be viewed as an attempt by someone to control the flow of information. The censorship issue has always been a critical test of a government, and propaganda remains a powerful weapon around the world.

Sam Nujomo, the leader of SWAPO, is still the president of Namibia, a country that seems to be progressing well by U.S., United Nations and its own standards. Namibians are still very conscious of that border and still view the area as a source of potential trouble. I'm not sure who or what is behind the quashing of this book. A number of ex-South African soldiers I have spoken with, who were involved one way or another in that bush war refered to it as their "Nam."

It's not clear to me why all this is so complicated, except that the U.S. and the U.N. were on the side of SWAPO, and Hooper's book is very anti-SWAPO. He has a lot of negative things to say about the United Nations, which are also now being said in various struggles around the world in which the U.N. has become involved.

Hooper's book is exciting and well written and deals with the author's observations on the cruelty and corruptness of SWAPO and the communist fighters, as contrasted with the bravery and competence of Koevoet and how racially integrated the Namibians and the South Africans were. But there is not one word in Hooper's book(s) about women combatants.

Later, while still in Windhoek, I saw a powerful and disturbing documentary about Nimibian women soldiers made by the Namibia Film Corporation as "a tribute to women soldiers in the struggle for freedom." It showed how they fought and were tortured and not given counseling, and how they developed "women's survival skills." It showed a number of women who now work for the Namibian Broadcasting Company being trained by SWAPO in Angola in 1978. Several were trained in film production and videography, skills that the survivors are now using.

For me, the documentary was both fascinating and horrifying. At times the film had the twinge of propaganda, but the struggles were real, with the same kind of horror that Hooper described. I was profoundly aware that many of women in the film were missing limbs and helpless at certain levels—and still under forty years old, which meant that some were teenagers when fighting. Some were still beautiful and clear headed. I also learned that some older Herero women had fought against the British years before, and after being shot at and bombed, sometimes wounded or killed, were exiled to the Seychelle Islands.

Once again I thought of Betsy Graves Reyneau, who, prior to becoming a famous painter, had gone to prison in the struggle to get American women the right to vote. Many of the women in the American suffrage movement were educated, articulate middle- and upper-class women, so the police didn't dare beat them. But when some of the women went on hunger strikes, the authorities did tie them down and force-feed them so they wouldn't die or look emaciated when they were released. An ignominious period in American history. I try to pass on to my kids, and to anyone who will listen, the attitude of sticking up for what you know is right, even though it may cost you dearly.

What with all of the histories and the problems, I continuously marvel that most African people don't seem to be filled with rage and the desire for vengeance. They just want to get on with a good life, which, typically the opportunists and the greedy mess up.

Scenery and animal pictures are incredible public relations tools for Namibia, and also there are some luxurious hotels and resorts in remote places in Namibia. Seeping into the travel videos and brochures are pictures of the new Windhoek Country Club, built by aggressive developers from South Africa (Stocks and Stocks Construction, which had just been upgraded on the Johannesburg Stock Exchange) with the principal purpose of promoting a gambling industry.

I took a shuttle bus from the Kalahari Sands Hotel, the expensive and only big multi-star hotel in downtown Windhoek, to the Country Club, which was another big public hotel a few miles out of town. The exterior resembled a Las Vegas gambling casino, thank God without the huge, ostentatious exterior lighting. The inside had typical thick patterned carpets, liveried bellhops, paintings, square pillars and gold lions—someone's idea of plush, not mine.

The classically huge gambling room with no clocks and zillions of slots and tables has the same depressing collection of people as any casino. Often desperate-looking people, mainly black in this part of the world, crowded into the change line with wadded up bills to get tokens or coins, blowing their small paychecks in desperate hopes of getting rich. As was true not only in Nevada and on the numerous Indian reservation gambling establishments that had sprung up all over the United States, it was the poorest people and those who could least afford to lose what little money they had. But they did. Compulsive gambling was beginning to be recognized as a social ill in Namibia as it was everywhere. When the addiction of a person with a little money is coupled with a smart and avaricious facility for extracting it, the gambler and the society deteriorate as the selfish prosper.

In anticipation of my trip to Africa I had done much reading, talking, studying and thinking. Our National Public Radio had been doing a number of stories about Africa, and when one day it was announced that there would be an interview with several people from Namibia, I wrote down the address and sent away for a copy of the tape. The tape said it was an interview with Mosé Tjitendero, the speaker of the Namibian Parliament. I decided to take it with me and give it to him if I could. But another German problem arose for me.

I was asked to look up an old friend of an acquaintance in Tucson; so dutifully I phoned her and was somewhat stunned by the inquisitorial barrage about where I was staying, how much did it cost, how many rooms were there, who ran it, was it clean, did they have mixed race people staying there, how big was my room and on and on. Eventually I said rather crisply that I would like to meet her for luncheon. She instantly suggested the most expensive German restaurant in town, and when I met the tight-lipped woman with the bleached blond hair pulled back tightly into a bun, I had an inkling of what was coming. I said that in my Tucson friend's honor, I would like her to be my guest. It was such a hot day that I simply wanted tea and a green salad, but I told her to have whatever she wanted. We could see the size of the salads on the next table, and they looked adequate to me. But no, she ordered a green salad and a chicken salad and wanted strudel for desert. We both just barely finished the green salad, so she had the chicken salad put in a box and nibbled at the strudel before putting it in the box as well.

I saw a sign across the patio saying "Stock Exchange," and said I wanted to peek in. "Now why would you want to do that?" she asked accusingly. I was about to say "None of your damn business," but simply said I'd be right back.

It turned out there was a staff of two girls and they didn't really have an exchange per se. No trading floor or ticker tapes, but there was some trading in a few South African stocks through a local dealer—but they expected the exchange to grow fantastically in the next year.

The blond was fidgeting when I got back, and again got inquisitorial. I wasn't going to put up with more of the same, so I said I was going to parliament—would she like to go. *Parliament?* she said sarcastically. No, she had never been, but did I realize how corrupt and incompetent this government was? But that she would drive me there because it was too far to walk. I said it was not too far to walk, but that I would appreciate a ride. My God, what a negative person. Later I found an earlier laptop note to myself saying "I have a feeling that she is not a nice person."

The security guards at the Parliament building were uniformed, armed and stood stiffly. My "companion" was rude and bossy, but to no avail. We were escorted up the stairs to the press box, but the fierce woman guard (with gun) said there were no seats and that we would have to wait until someone left. In loud stage whispers to me the blond went on with her barrage of disparaging remarks about how arrogant "these people" were and about how she had so many better things to do, like translate documents into German for some local businessmen to be faxed to businesses in Germany.

When finally we were seated, I was fascinated by a protracted speech by a white conservative member about family values and how men were the traditional heads of the families and women should obey them and people should not live in sin and not have abortions and so forth and so on.

It was all very orderly—boring, yes, but orderly. I began studying the stiff, uncomfortable, freshly upholstered seats, the beautiful detailing on the formal columns of this stately old building that had served as the seat of the German colonial government. Lots of ironies.

Shortly my companion poked me rudely and said, "Let's go." I said she could go, but I was staying. She left. What a relief. The chicken salad had begun to leak through the plastic bag onto her skirt, but I said nothing.

The next speaker was a round black woman who spoke very articulately and courteously about not disagreeing with the previous speaker about the importance of family, but in this day there were women who headed households and should be afforded the same rights as men. I closed my eyes and imagined I was in the States.

As I left, I politely asked the guard where I could find the office of the speaker, explaining that I had a cassette tape to give to him. She seemed startled by my American accent and immediately became a softer, more helpful person, instructing another guard (also armed) to take me there. We walked down long marble halls, through beautiful wide wooden doors and stood face to face with the receptionist's large desk—just like being in Washington. I explained my "gift." The receptionist asked me if I would like to meet "Mr. Speaker." I was thrilled, so we set up an appointment at noon two days later.

Mosé Tjitendero (the correct spelling of Chitendero, which was how his name was spelled on the label of the tape), a large, black, very distinguished, graceful "elder statesman" type, rose to greet me as I was escorted by his administrative assistant into the large, tastefully decorated office full of oriental rugs and fine furniture befitting a high government official. His administrative assistant, a bright and articulate pale-colored young woman (I was not sure if she is white or coloured) sat on a sofa with a notebook. The soft-spoken, American-educated Mr. Speaker and I talked interestingly (for me, at least) for forty-five minutes about everything from desert management, optimum populations for drainage basins and illegal immigration to smoking and illiteracy. He said they had a ninety percent alcoholism rate in Namibia. I was so shocked I asked him to repeat it, which he did.We talked about mineral rights and the government's position on denying the ISCOR Mining Corporation mineral rights, which the company contends will throw it into bankruptcy. He simply shrugged his shoulders.

A few days earlier the Nigerian government had quickly

tried and executed nine men, including a famous writer, Ken Serewewo, to the horror of the United Nations and many world governments. I asked him if Namibia had a position on what was going on in Nigeria. He said the minister of communications was working on a way to talk with the defiant Nigerian government. I forgot to ask him if Namibia had a policy on the death penalty.

Democracy is a fragile thing in emerging nations, of which Africa has so many. Mr. Speaker told me he had heard that Islamic militants have vowed to wreck the upcoming Algerian elections, which saddened him.

Tjitendero was so educated, so gentle and articulate and could explain his global view so well that it was hard for me to visualize him as one of Hooper's SWAPO villains; but war does hideous things to even the nicest people.

He told me about some recent trade agreements that Namibia had concluded with Luxembourg—probably not too large in my view, he said, "knowing how Americans think," but it was important to Namibia. He smiled.

I told him about the Namibian WorldTeach, the Harvard Institute for International Development program that I had first experienced in Ecuador. He knew of the program and was interested in their literacy training efforts in Namibia and South Africa and wanted to learn more. I gave him the name and phone number of Michael Armstrong, the local field coordinator, which the A.A. dutifully wrote down.

On purpose I did not bring up the two expensive Mercedes sitting side by side with their drivers in the parking lot, like a matched pair of bay horses waiting to whisk important officials off to wherever. My blond "friend" had pointed them out as symbols of how the country was going to hell in a handbasket.

I asked about the priorities of his government. "Everything is a burning issue—education, housing, health. We have no time to prioritize." He continued, "But among African nations, we are the last born, the youngest child, and we are trying to learn from the failures of others."

We had talked for about forty-five minutes. I was beginning to feel guilty about taking so much time and said so. Tjitendero smiled graciously, rose and gave me a slip of paper with his home phone number on it. "If you have a chance, call my wife. She's from Davis, California, and would be delighted to make a cup of tea for you."

My first few days in Namibia had been spent in the elegant home of a friend of a friend in one of the newest and nicest suburbs of Windhoek. The large, charming recently remodelled house had some definite African accents, like beautiful carvings of animals in native woods, but even more German memorabilia, including a crisp copy of *Mein Kampf* in the center of the bookcase. My own family had Hitler's book of plans, and had read it when it first came out; but the book seemed to have a different meaning here—almost an uncomfortable symbolism.

I was struck by how American or German everything in the house was, including almost every known kitchen appliance, a stereo and CD players. The radio was always turned to Radio 99, the contemporary hip (but definitely *not* hip-hop) radio station. After Hootie and the Blowfish, Michael Jackson, Michael Bolton and other current favorites, at least one German drinking song or accordion or oom-pah record was played every hour.

An enormous TV dominated the living room, but there were only two channels in town. It is *so nice* not having commercials break up a program. I often retired to my room to give my hostess time to herself. I could hear Oprah Winfry, Melrose Place and Baywatch, which were her favorite programs. Choices weren't great, but her choices temporarily surprised me until I learned that this educated, articulate, attractive person had never been in a public library, didn't know any or care to know any black people and and openly didn't care for things African. Family, schooling and friends were 100 percent German, and she was not averse to expressing her contempt for people of color and an intense dislike of African music.

Above and beyond all, I was overwhelmed by the household security. There was a high, solid perimeter wall with glass shards embedded in the top and an electronic opener to slide the heavy gates into slots in the wall so that the car could enter. There was another opener for steel-roller garage doors, several security systems, including one for the heavy metal screen door, then double keys for deadbolts on the house doors. When inside, even if the doors or windows were open, you couldn't get out because of bars and locked gates. Beautiful, tasteful and handsome as the house was, I felt like I was in an elegant prison. I haven't felt that "secure" since being in Germany shortly after World War II.

News traveled fast in Namibia. The small populations everywhere lead to small-town characteristics. Everyone seems to know everybody else's business with gossip reigning and secrets violated. My host's husband had been killed in a tragic small-plane crash shortly after she found out she was pregnant. En route to her parents' isolated but prosperous farm when she was eight months pregnant, she had had a terrible roll-over car accident on a remote gravel road and lain unconscious for quite a while. She had been badly bruised, cut and scraped, with several broken bones, but there wasn't even a scratch around her midriff, where the baby resided. It was hours before anyone discovered her, and by the time she got to her parents' farm, people were calling from as far away as the coast to extend condolences on the death of the baby. Her beautiful daughter was born a month later.

Windhoek is surrounded by small, bare mountains. You can easily walk to places where you can look out over the city and see that it is an urban dot in a sea of tan, arid desert. The population of about 200,000, not counting the uncountable people in the adjacent shanty towns, is the cosmopolitan capital of a vast country (half a million square miles—about the size of France) with a total population of under 1.5 million. It's an interesting and old town with industrial parks to the north and south. It contains the very contemporary Post Street Mall with its sophisticated shops, fine restaurants, bookstores, a computer store, boutiques, copy shops, ice cream stores, beautiful displays of local crafts and artwork for sale, public artworks and a fascinating display of some of the larger known meteorites that have hit the country.

Nike-clad tourists and people in identifiably ethnic dress from all over the world perambulate among the displays of hand-carved rhinos and giraffes, jewelry, baskets and pots. There were also wads of teens, black, white and coloured, in T-shirts with the pictures and messages ubiquitous in that age group. Rigid local white women in discreet floral dresses walk beside numerous black Herero women with their distinctive tall headpieces which were miraculously wrapped scarves that resembled tall flat-topped hats with large points sticking out over each shoulder. The bright calico-type materials of the dresses and the headdresses were a legacy of Victorian-era missionary modesty, which dictated the high necks and eight petticoats under the gorgeous colorful skirts even on days when literally an egg would fry on any exterior surface. These women were proud, elegant and private. In hindsight, I think my biggest single regret of the whole trip was not talking with some of the older Herero women about Reverend Michael Scott.

The three-story Wernhil Center, adjacent to the mall, had a super-market and escalators where young men checked out all the young women who rode up and down the escalators expecting to be watched. There were many shops, including a chain bookstore, a liquor store, ice cream shop where I got my daily cone, and a public toilet—very important information when you are travelling.

Christmas was approaching. I ducked into the mall to get out of the stifling afternoon, which was similar to a light blue Tucson midsummer day. As a dreary version of "Jingle Bells" droned in the background, I watched very black men in royal blue coveralls delicately untangling a string of Christmas lights to adorn a gigantic fake fluffy green wreath. Long cables hanging down from the roof suggested that the wreath would be tugged high to the wall in back of the large fake Christmas tree heavily decked with red bows. It was somewhat cooler in the shopping center, but still just plain hot. I was numbed by the irony of tinny choruses of "Dashing through the snow...." engulfing slow-moving people mopping their brows.

A number of medical facilities were sprinkled around Windhoek, including a famous old hospital with a huge stork for a weather vane. When a baby was born, they hoisted either a pink or a blue flag, so that everyone in town knew the gender of the infant. Everyone already knew who was having the baby.

There was one huge world-class hotel, the Kalahari Sands—notwithstanding the fact that the Kalahari Desert was in South Africa, not Namibia, and there was the national university, and a national library under construction. Windhoek had fancy suburbs, slummy suburbs, embassies from around the world, a couple of radio stations and a couple of newspapers.

The main drag of downtown Windhoek, Independence Avenue, some big stores and banks and office buildings, travel agencies, a gun shop, a *biltong* shop and a Chinese restaurant where I had ostrich foo-yung. Not bad.

Crime definitely exists in Namibia, much of it relating to mineral resources, especially diamonds. Namibia has large deposits of diamonds, including placer deposits or stones just lying around on the ground and the ocean floor. It is a heavily regulated industry, and certain areas, especially along the Skeleton Coast, are restricted and patrolled. The De Beers empire of South Africa only has partial control of the Namibian resources, a rare situation when it comes to diamonds. But that's how the government, which wants a cut, fights to keep things.

One day I walked into a very fancy jewelry store on Independence Avenue and said cheerily, "I would like to see some uncut diamonds, please." The elegant clerk's face darkened, and his jaw dropped. The guy looked at me as though I were some sort of lunatic—like I had walked into the police station and said "I've never seen 10 pounds of cocaine. Would you please show me some? I'm thinking about buying some of those little baggies of it as souvenirs for my friends."

Basically that's what I *had* said. Apparently it is illegal to solicit to buy raw diamonds, and it is absolutely illegal to own one, even if you find it in your own front yard. The clerk realized that I was completely ignorant of this and gave me a stern lecture on never saying that again, at least in public or to strangers.

As I was exploring the many interesting little side streets of Windhoek, which, like those of most towns, often held treasure spots for those who sought them out, I became aware of being followed by a man. I gripped my purse tightly in front of me and walked firmly and confidently on, almost striding, which is a neat trick for us short-legged ones. Soon he was walking sideways beside me, with bent knees, palms upturned and the customary language of the beggar about buying bread for his wife and children. I had been cautioned about giving in, because generosity almost always was to maintain an alcohol problem.

He was dreadfully persistent, so I stopped, turned, looked him straight in the eye and said *no*. He dropped his hands to his side, stood up straight (much taller than me) looked me straight in the eye and said, "That's why we kill people like you."

Very taken aback, I simply turned, stood as straight and tall as I could and strode away from him, not daring to look back. Fortunately, the buildings abutted the edge of the sidewalk on that little street and there were lots of people.

Suddenly, to my amazement, out of a doorway stepped the woman named Gertrude whom I had ridden up with on the bus from Cape Town. "I was going to call you," she said. "And here you are. I have it all arranged with the editor. You are to be interviewed for next week's paper. Come with me." Before I knew what was happening, I was sitting in the office of Christine Visser, an attractive, bright twenty-five-year-old reporter/editorialist for the *TEMPO* which, she said, was one of several owned by her boss, which were the "opposition press" to the one-party SWAPO-dominated government. She was a European-educated Afrikaner professional woman with impeccable English. We got along immediately and talked about all sorts of things, including spessartite, a rare orange garnet, which her boyfriend and his partners took to the world-famous Tucson, Arizona, Gem and Mineral show every year. Small world!

The next Sunday there was a picture of me and a nice article with the headline DESERT PERSON VISITS NAMIBIA.

I am a desert person by nature, so the long drive from Windhoek through surrounding arid landscapes en route to the Namib National Park and the great dunes was of interest to me. But the loud conversation of my travelling companions, four fat German tourists with big bellies and big cameras, bluntly and repeatedly announced it as unpleasant. To a person who loves green trees, flowers and bushes, or a prosperous farm, rolling green hills, this desert would at least be baffling. But why then did these tourists insist on frequent stops to take pictures and ceremoniously examine little stones with their handlenses and pull up tiny plants to examine while bitching to the driver about driving too fast and complaining about everything from the condition of the vehicle to the scrawniness of the sparse vegetation? I viewed them with the same annoyance as most foreigners view the braggadocio of a Texan or, as a well-known South African singer put it, "those bands of Americans from their mid-west who constantly whine in e-flat minor." So many travellers forget that they are in someone else's country, and it should be accepted for what it is.

Our lodgings, the small Namib Nauklift Lodge—in the middle of nowhere on the edge of nothing except the incredible dunes—were more elegant than I expected or needed, but a treat. We had been politely but repeatedly cautioned about not wasting water. To my delight I spotted a small swimming pool. I put on my suit and rushed over, only to find that it was so cold that I didn't go in. Back in my room I stared out the picture windows trying to grasp distances. Later I learned that hillocks that seemed like one could stroll over to them after dinner were ten miles away.

I drifted toward an opening in a huge curved stone wall that resembled many of the traditional kraals (corrals) I had seen. It also served as a windbreak in this barren land where the wind rules. Dinner was to be held there, and some people had already arrived and were standing around drinking. I overheard a giant of a black man, one of the guides, conversing in perfect German to another group of Germans who were leaving the next morning. Several round black women in immaculate white dresses and aprons and caps were busy cooking on the huge permanent grill. Namibia, even more than South Africa, is a very meat eating country (it's easier to raise sheep than lettuce), and often the meat is cooked on a grill, called a *braai* (pronounced "bri," as in "Brian").

Occasionally, one of the Germans would break into English, I think for my sake, with some snotty remark about how the Namibian beer of course couldn't compare with German beer, but that it was passable. While this was probably true, the manner in which it was said was getting to me. It didn't need to be said at all.

A forever memorable highlight (among many) for me came after dinner, when by the glowing light of the coals and two smaller fires two of the round cooks and a beautiful long-legged young waitresses in tight shorts began to dance and sing on the surrounding high round boulders, accompanied by a CD on a boom box. The lighting and shadows were wonderfully mysterious.

Because I had stayed a few extra days so as to spend more time in the dunes, I was to drive back to Windhoek with a different driver than I had come with. He had a huge scar on his elbow from an auto accident, but he could straighten his arm and was a wonderful driver on the winding mountainous dirt roads in this very unforgiving terrain. In both Namibia and South Africa, horrendous automobile accidents are a huge cause of death and maiming—as I had already found out.

I had a different set of German traveling companions on the way back—a rather handsome retired orthodontist, who had been an officer in the German army (and to me talked like he was still a Nazi) and his slender, officious wife, who professed to have trouble with her spine and several other major maladies that required her to sit in the front seat (where she nagged the driver incessantly). There was a cute young Swiss guy and his silent girlfriend and me. The driver I had come down with had been conducting tours in the dunes and was deadheading back to Windhoek with us. When the dentist realized that we were to have a black passenger, he very pointedly placed his knapsack in such a way as to tell everyone that the man was to sit in the back with the luggage. The hostilities were unspoken but mutual, and when we would have an occasional rest stop, the two black drivers would dutifully pass out cans of tonic or soda or bottled water and then separate themselves to converse in Herero.

Namibia, despite its intrigues and complexities, is the most "laid-back" country I have ever been in. In addition to its incredible endowment of rare mineral resources, it looks in large part to tourism as a future economic base. There are those who would also like to see gambling as a major industry. But as elsewhere in the world, the scarcity of water will be the limiting factor. There just isn't a lot of water there, ground or surface. To the horror and dismay of ecologists and bird lovers worldwide, as well as of the natives and others, there is serious talk of drawing water from the Okavango River on the northeastern border. The Okavango delta is one of the richest and most beautiful wetlands in the world.

Perhaps two dozen companies are actively exploring seismically and geologically for water deposits. But barring something as yet unknown, that procedure, by definition, has its limits. Places like the Namib dunes make one realize how puny even a collection of smart people using the best instruments and knowledge are when going head to head with nature. Everything but the dunes can be flushed away in a few hours by a flash flood or a heavy wind. The dunes simply change.

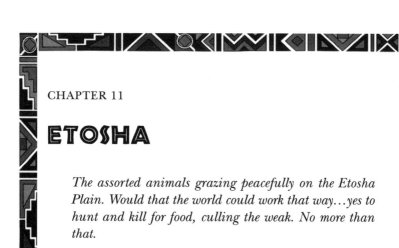

CHAPTER 11

ETOSHA

The assorted animals grazing peacefully on the Etosha Plain. Would that the world could work that way...yes to hunt and kill for food, culling the weak. No more than that.

From laptop notes to myself

In many countries, including Namibia, bed and breakfast places and pensions are a good way to live inexpensively with some order; predictable and secure. Breakfast is commonly served for a couple of hours; tables have been set the night before, and you sit and eat with whomever shows up. It was interesting to me to meet so many people with so many stories; two girls from New York who were affiliated with WorldTeach Namibia; three black public health nurses from a remote village in the Caprivi Strip; a young couple from France who travelled on a motorcycle with their two young children in a sidecar; a German doctor who gave me the clipping about homosexuality in black tribes (quoted elsewhere) and two attractive but secretive brothers from Liberia, with whom I peripherally became embroiled in a frighteningly illegal scheme.

The owner/manager and "able-to-do-everything" person at the Pension Alexander on Beethovenstrasse, where I stayed for several weeks, is named Alex, as was my son, so we instantly had something besides business to talk about. In the B&B business one must be cordial and efficient. But the delightful discovery for me was that, unlike most Germans I had met, Alex had a terrific sense of humor. His Germanness did cause mild trouble with some of his help, usually black people under twenty who had been born somewhere else in the vast country. For example, they simply didn't seem to grasp the importance to him of placing the spoon at the exact spot on the table where he wanted it. I teased him a bit about unnecessary precision, he teased me about drinking so much fruit juice at breakfast, and quickly we got to laughing about all sorts of things, including the spoons. He did lighten up a bit, but I had to agree after a week that the fifteen-year-old maid apparently did not comprehend that cleaning the bathroom did not just mean folding wet towels, exploring the medicine chest and changing the toothbrush from one side of the basin to the other.

Alex, a tall, attractive man in his mid-thirties, with a smart, beautiful wife and a brand-new baby, had the ongoing necessity to speak several languages, and he was eager for assistance with his English. My pleasure. I was at Pension Alexander on and off for a month, so gradually we became good chatting buddies. He loved American country-western music, as did I. We talked about politics, religion and life matters, and answered each other's questions. His English improved enormously. To me the ultimate sign of the grasp of another language was being able to tell jokes and understand humor. He could, and we did.

Religion was strong in Namibia, with many more Lutherans and Catholics and fewer Anglicans than in South Africa. Grace was regularly said by many, and never once did I hear a swear word in a public place. One day, in a totally innocent context, Alex used the "F" word, often considered obscene in English. I brought him up short, and although he was embarrassed when I explained, we both thought it was funny and he promised to be careful. He said I needed to teach him to swear a bit in English.

Days earlier we had agreed that one of the guests was a real bitch, and Alex tried to teach me how to say some gross phrase in German about dogs and bitches, but it didn't take on my linguistically shallow ear. So with examples of context situations, appropriate uses, what is a proper audience, etc., I taught him to say "son of a bitch." He wanted me to write it down, which I did. He loved it. He picked up the paper and walked around the dining room, as though rehearsing a school play, saying, "Son of a bitch, son of a bitch, son of a bitch," with different intonations, facial expressions and gestures. I said, *"Stop, stop!"* But the sorcerer's apprentice was off and running.

He asked for more. I said no. Later we encountered each other on the patio and smiled that subtle smile that one smiles when sharing a secret. As he turned to go inside to attend to his baby, I saw a small pistol stuck in his belt in the middle of his back.

Later I went to the lounge to watch the eight o'clock news in English. The two Liberian brothers I had seen earlier were already seated in the lounge when I appeared. Usually I had the place to myself and took my laptop to catch up on my notes as I watched. The brothers courteously said hello in English but said nothing further except to each other in some other language.

The only vacant seat at the breakfast next morning was next to them. To me they looked like college students, so I inquired whether they were on "holiday" (vacation). One started to say something, and immediately the apparently older one butted in and took over. "Business," he said abruptly and went back to eating. Trying to lighten up the conversation a bit, I politely asked what kind of business. Again the bigger one interrupted the other and said "transportation." I could tell he was lying. He sensed that I knew that he was lying and modified his answer by saying "automobiles." I said nothing more.

The next morning they both showed up in expensive and fashionable gold-rimmed glasses. I had never seen either wear glasses before. That night in the TV room, they seemed as interested in the news as I was, and then as a spot about trouble in Liberia began, they watched intensely and jabbered with each other.

I had said nothing until then and simply commented that I had heard a little bit about trouble in Liberia on my short-wave radio. "Looks bad," I said. The older one looked at me intently and said, "Civil war. Our father is a banker, and we're here to tend to business."

I didn't see them for a day or two until one more breakfast as they were getting up from the table—and then they disappeared. Several nights later I had the television room to myself, and as I was about to leave, a very troubled Alex came out of the kitchen and asked if I would look at something for him.

He took me into the office, which was filled with a peculiar, unpleasant chemical odor. Sitting on the floor was a box about the size of a carton of apples, covered in stars-and-stripes wrapping paper, with a small door on the top with a keyhole. On the side of the box it said "Five million U.S. dollars." With an ordinary type of key that is used to "lock" closets and drawers, he opened the top. He said that he had been told it was a vault of "breeze money," whatever that was. The box was lined with cotton batting, which was permeated with a nearly overpowering chemical, and currency-size pieces of gray paper were piled up in the center to the top edge. Alex showed me some crudely printed papers, which supposedly were authentication of some sort. A sheet of typing paper with a ghastly off-register photo of some woman's face captioned "Head of chemical department of the U.S. Government." I couldn't believe how poor the printing, the paper, and the red, white and blue colors were. I told him we didn't have a chemical department, per se. Another letterhead said "Federal Reserved [with a d] Bank, Washington, D.C. New York" followed by five digits, supposedly a zip code, which I knew belonged to neither New York nor Washington.

Alex produced a little vial of orange fluid, and with a piece of cotton began rubbing it on one of the gray pieces of paper. A picture of a U.S. hundred-dollar bill began to appear. It was just a picture, not a real bill, but he assured me that he had seen them do it, and a real hundred-dollar bill emerged. "Who are they?" I asked incredulously. "Those guys from Liberia," he said. I couldn't believe what I was seeing and hearing, let alone smelling.

Alex was not a dumb person, but how would he have known whether we had a chemical department? The thing that set him thinking was that five million dollars would probably be in a bigger box.

He flung open the closet doors, and there were all the young men's clothes. I recognized some of the shirts. On the floor were several duffles, including one that had been used to carry the box of breeze money. He opened his safe, and there were copies of the brothers' passports and the gold-rim glasses.

A prudent inn keeper got paid in advance. The young men had paid for a couple of days, and then paid for a couple more but became three days behind with their payments. Alex went to their room to collect. Apparently they were quite startled to see him and said they were about to come over to the office to discuss an investment with him. Their father was president of a bank, and there was much profit to be made by a person like Alex because of the unrest in their country.

They showed him the box and washed away the coating on a bill with the chemical, producing a crisp, clean, genuine C-note, as nearly as Alex could tell. They said that one must only take out one or two "bills" at a time from the top of the pile to wipe with the solution, and they or someone else would be around periodically to sell him more of the chemical for forty dollars a bottle. Alex thought the invention was interesting, but he said he wanted the rent money right then. Apparently they hardened in a way that he perceived as threatening. He whipped out the pistol from the back of his belt and told them to get out and not come back until they had the money they owed him. He moved all of their belongings into the office, where he placed them under lock and key.

What did I think? he asked. Apparently my eyes were still as big as saucers, and I told him I had a duty to go to the American embassy first thing in the morning and to please give me a couple of the bills and the printed material. Sheepishly he complied.

Traveling with jewelry is usually not a good idea, but I did have a string of pearls and matching earrings. I put on a blue dress, stockings, white heels and my pearls. Alex showed me on a map where the embassy was.

It was too early for a bus, and a cab would take an hour to get to the pension. The embassy opened at eight. Alex had to stay to serve breakfast to the other guests, otherwise he would have driven me. I said not to worry, that it wasn't all that far and I didn't mind walking. Already it was hot, and when I began to feel that I had walked too far, I realized that I was on a parallel street. So I doubled back and walked down the hill to the embassy. As I walked through the gate, as sometimes happened when traveling, I was absolutely thrilled to see the stars and stripes. I felt so patriotic.

I walked in at about 8:10. Embassies are like fortresses in

most countries, and while this one was small, there were armed guards, bullet-proof glass, metal detectors and the rest. I got to an inner desk. Two guys with coffee cups were leisurely chatting. One of them deigned to inquire, "Can we do something for you, Miss?"

I thought small obscenities and then in a loud voice said I would like to see the chief security officer about fraud, counterfeiting and perhaps more. The place sprung into action.

Momentarily I was greeted by a James Bond adonis—head of security. I asked that we be alone, and he escorted me out to the patio where we talked and I showed him the papers. He said he needed to call the Namibian police and that they would check it out right away. I asked if I could have a ride back. Just as we drove up to the gate at the pension, a black detective from the Namibian police drove up. We were introduced, and I directed them to the office. We all understood that I was no longer needed, so I headed back to my room. Little did I know what they would find in the office.

That evening as I was watching the news, Alex came in and explained that very morning, soon after I left for the embassy, the brothers had returned with a big gruff man who identified himself as being with the United Nations delegation (Alex wasn't sure which nation the man represented). The guy wanted to pay Alex what was due with a check and have him hand over everything. Alex said no, he wanted cash. Things got ugly, but Alex held his ground. The man left, and the brothers sat nervously in the office as the U.N. guy went out to get the cash. He had just come back, and they were talking and counting the rent money, when in walked the embassy official and the detective.

The detective arrested the kids, had the U.N. guy also go down "to the station" with them, and confiscated the box of breeze money and related materials. The police called Alex later in the day to say that they all had been deported and, he was told, would never set foot in Namibia again.

The next day I left early for a guided trip to the coast and up through the north of the country to the Etosha Pan. Except for Alex, I had about had it with Germans; so imagine my horror when I got into the tour company's combi and found a German guide and five German tourists. But my "second chance" viewing of situations seemed to be standing me in good stead so far. The week-long trip was one of the most delightful, interesting and hilariously funny times of my life. As always I was astonished by what humor can do for a situation.

The combi was an hour late because for some reason they assumed that I, like all but one of the others, was staying at the Kalahari Sands. A head or two might have rolled at the travel agency, but we were long gone.

Everyone spoke at least adequate English, and a dashingly attractive, very sophisticated couple spoke almost without accent. The guide, Peter (ah, Peter, with whom in a day or two I was exchanging bawdy jokes and conspiring to play practical jokes on the other members of the group) was a Namibian but had been an intelligence officer in the South African army for seven years. He was quite secretive about many things, and it became clear that he wasn't going to clarify. So I just had to accept numerous inconsistencies in his stories.

We were en route to the famous and historic German colonial town of Swakopmund on the coast. The main road we traveled is a two-lane road that divides the Namib Nauklift Park from the Skeleton Coast Park. Distances were very great in Namibia, and you simply didn't pass by a little town or even a crossroads gas station. There weren't any. The emptiness was part of the beauty, and we made several stops to see the rare sights like the primitive two-leaf welwitchia plants, perhaps 500 years old, lying close to the ground in the pulsating heat of the midday sun. The terrain was a flat beige plain that ran to the skyline, with large lone trees of the sycamore family here and there. We had a box lunch under one. It was amazing how the temperature dropped to nearly tolerable in the shade. I asked about the two anomalous pieces of fence, each perhaps six feet high and three feet wide that formed a "V" a few hundred feet from our tree. A grin that I would come to know well crept across Peter's face. He stared at me and waited long enough for me to ask again. He bowed graciously, gestured with his left hand and said "For ladies," and gestured with his right hand "For gentlemen." I blushed, and he and the others laughed.

Without warning to the first-time visitor, we suddenly were on the brink of a vast series of canyons, cliffs and plateaus with pock marks that resembled the surface of the moon. Peter announced that the American moon landing was a hoax, and that they had filmed it here. I was catching on, and simply said, "Oh." (But I have to secretly admit that it did look like a possibility.)

One of our party was a botanist. To proudly demonstrate how full of life this moonscape was, Peter plucked a dead-looking, ratty little piece of lichen from a rock and told us to watch how it would come to life with just a little water. I accused him of using bubbly soda water to make it jump around, which he vigorously denied until he saw all of us laughing. Quickly he shook the bottle and pretended to spray it at me and then went back to his demonstration. Desert vegetation and the bizarre but abundant animal and insect life was in a class by itself, and Peter knew a lot about it, which was interesting for all of us.

The minute we crossed over a small sandy rise and started to glide down many miles of sandy road, the temperature dropped dramatically. Sea breezes from the cold Atlantic were ahead. Just before town we passed a new gambling resort like the Windhoek Country Club. We encountered the same attitudes and same types of people, high rollers, pseudo-high rollers, silly tourists, compulsive gamblers and the desperately hopeful and the desperately poor were entering and leaving.

After a couple of historic statue-and-plaque stops and a swift drive around the small, methodically laid out town and along the waterfront past the so-called fancy (very expensive) hotels, we checked into the Hansa Hotel. It is a three-star in the five-star system used throughout the country. I had stayed at a number of one-star hotels which were perfectly satisfactory, but this was indeed charming and very European—wood panelling, good wall coverings, formal dining room, liveried bellhops and the like. And the rooms (all facing a charming flower-filled courtyard) had big beds! I was wearying of the little, skinny, sagging, lumpy or cement-like beds that I found in most of the places I stayed (including homes). And here there was a telephone that actually worked. An export-import friend in the States had asked me to call one of her suppliers of wood carvings and fabrics, which led to an interesting conversation about Namibian economics.

We dressed for dinner, meaning we wore clean slacks and tops—in southern Africa they called this attire "Smart Casual." Peter, a large man in his early forties, smoked way too much and was developing a characteristic beer belly. He always was present for the cocktail hour (and made sure that there always was a cocktail hour). He drank beer, lots of beer, always ate black bread and lots of smoked meat. A fresh vegetable never crossed his lips as far as I could observe. He never drank during the day but made up for it at night. He spoke in German most of the time, so I was always seated near him so he could translate for me. The others were discreetly sipping wine, and out of the blue Peter said he wanted to buy a bottle of wine for the two of us. We shared a bottle of one of the world-class South African wines. I knew he didn't make a lot of money, so the next night I offered to do the same. It got to be a delightful habit, to the entertainment of our colleagues, who drank modestly, if at all. Some of my fellow travelers were eager to speak in English part of the time, and to my astonishment I was getting the gist of the German chatter, based on the context of the situation.

The attractive young waitresses were black women, each with an infinite number of tiny braids. Their braids were so well ordered with such shine. Needless to say I was startled when Peter told me that the hair was made of plastic. Oh well—youthful fashion statement and very pretty, I thought.

The ocean is the ocean, and next morning it was foggy and cold. But we left at about six for the beaches below Walvis Bay to see the flamingos. I never knew there were so many flamingos in the world. Enormous flocks of long necks on pink puff balls perched on stick-like legs took breakfast from the mud flats of the outgoing tide. Then a few hundred would rise on their huge and increasingly graceful wings into the dissipating cloud cover into the blue sky. We were all breathless with awe.

Peter, in guide-like fashion, announced that the flamingos were pink because there was something akin to paprika in their food. I asked if they would get red and dance if they ate chili powder. He turned and quickly frowned, then smiled broadly as he saw the others chortling, and for the first time said to me,

"Oh, shut up," which got to be a catch phrase for all of us.

A couple of hours north of Swakopmund, after seemingly endless, trackless miles of sandy road, dunes on one side, ocean on the other and only one or two cars each hour, we came on a formal turnout and parking lot with a heavy stone wall paralleling the beach. Beyond the wall were what looked and sounded like a million seals, breeding, birthing, flopping around and doing all those things seals do on land. I was saddened to hear a couple of months later that a terrible storm had killed hundreds of baby seals, which had washed up on beaches to the south. I was afraid to think what it smelled like as the seals' odor was bad enough when they were alive.

Heading inland from the northern coast of Namibia was a peculiar experience of emptiness. I would see a little track of road ahead, but nothing else except bare, sandy plateaus and mountains. Nothing. To some of us the subtleties, patterns of light, colors and textures were very beautiful. Some of our party clearly didn't like it.

Gradually we rose into the high country of Damaraland. Peter would see things that none of us saw. Suddenly we would stop. He cut the engine and whispered, "Elephant tracks." Only after staring at the marks in the dirt road could I discern that they were round and about the size of an elephant's foot. That wasn't nearly as hard as seeing the zebra tracks or even the unusual little rodent tracks. Sure enough, beneath a distant tree was a motionless elephant. It is tempting to describe all of the plants and animals and environments, but it would take a lifetime.

Our lodgings at Khorixas were sort of 1930s Oklahoma highway-type white cabins with green tar paper roofs, leaky showers, sash windows and two-part doors with pointless locks. But that's what there was for lodgings in that part of the world. Drinks were incredibly expensive, so we skipped the wine that night. And besides, I was engrossed in conversation with a young fellow named Tony, a Qualified Conservationist (meaning he had a degree), who was the regional warden of Damaraland. With small government funding, donations and some support from an international conservation body he was doing an elephant census and was much involved with the Save the Rhino

Trust. He used a donated laptop to keep statistics, borrowed a plane (and pilot) to hustle equipment and services from a local vetenarian, and yes, they always needed money. But he seemed thrilled that someone would actually listen to him—and care.

The next day we drove past a "painted desert," which didn't reveal much color from a distance, and to a petrified forest. Both trips took a lot of patience, at least for me. The thirty-foot-long logs, now brilliant-colored stone were pretty impressive, as were stumps four feet across. One was struck with the span of world history and could fantasize about past forests and dinosaurs. After a professional lecture in German, which I didn't need translated because of previous geologic experience, everyone seemed to wander off on a separate path. Mine rose up a little hill overlooking the stark but beautiful peaceful emptiness which was so calming. Peter was sitting smoking on a petrified log. "This is really exciting," I said. Poor choice of words. While interesting, it was anything but exciting. We both burst out laughing.

Box lunches had been brought along from Khorixas, much too much food for one person, and there was nothing except an orange that would keep in the heat. Every day Peter would collect the extra sandwiches, eggs, meat, candy, fruit and other stuff and turn them over to natives who just happened to be nearby for some reason or other. A barefoot man led us up through a steep, rocky trail to amazingly detailed petroglyphs depicting many familiar and lots of unfamiliar animals. His family had a long heritage of living and hunting in these barren lands; but recently, guiding clumps of tourists to his ancestor's artworks was a vital part of his survival. In addition to the food, Peter slipped him some cash. I suggested that since the travel companies were making a mint off this place, they should chip in and build some protective shelters for the historical artworks, which clearly were suffering some weathering. He said the point had never come up but that he thought it was a good idea and would suggest it to the board of directors.

Etosha is a Namibian national park, a high, arid plane with scrubby bushes and thorny trees which are the essence of Africa to many people. The east and north is the blindingly white, sterile and featureless Etosha Pan leading to the pale blue sky. It has small and large herds of a dozen different sizes and types of antelope, anteaters, ostriches, armadillos, big cats, rhinos, little cats, wild dogs, hippos, zebras, wildebeests (blue and black), bugs and birds that defy description. Clumps of elephants discreetly moved away as we approached. There was no sign of humankind except the dirt road.

Earlier I mentioned the severe drought that had plagued southern Africa for many years. Water holes were drying up in the Etosha plain and pan and becoming small blue or gray disks on the pale, naked soil. They were hard to see in such a flat land, but somehow Peter knew where they all were. Before we could see the water, we could see the giraffes, maybe twenty of all ages, including some mere seven-foot-tall babies. We crept as close as we dared to the magic invisible line where we could be the closest without scaring them away. The silence was so overpowering that I didn't even want to swallow or chew my gum. When giraffes drank they spread their front legs far apart, and to my astonishment they seemed to dislocate their shoulder blades to be able to reach their mouths to the water. They drank for a long time and then struggled to reassemble themselves and stand upright again. Always there was one standing "on guard."

The stillness, the purity of the air and the experiences change one's life, or at least they did for me. It's an inner peace that is hard to explain. Several days of this quiet routine is anything but a routine when you suddenly encounter a band of curious baboons or a pack of hyenas following several big cats chasing a young wildebeest.

Tall thorn trees, trimmed on top by giraffes and on the bottom by anything that could reach, gave way to a flat, scrub-filled plain as we cruised along to our next lodgings. Every day was hot. We always had a couple of coolers with lots of small cans of tonic, tea, soda and bottled water. We had extra tires and gas, but this was a place I would not have liked to blow a head gasket.

After much thought I finally leaned over to Peter and said, "I'm hallucinating." He stopped the car gently but quickly, turned around and looked at me very seriously. "Hallucinating?" he asked with a worried tone. "Yes," I said. "Every bush looks like a toilet to me." Apparently everyone else felt the same. Peter sputtered and then laughed—"Boys to the left, girls to the right," he said, shaking his head.

We arrived in the lobby of the *five* star lodge in mid-afternoon, sweaty, dusty, tired and thirsty. The numerous busboys in their trim, sand colored shorts and cotton shirts with ironed creases on the short sleeves took our luggage to our individual elegant cool rooms after the manager had greeted us with large glasses of lemonade. There were four large, private, well-appointed rooms in each of the white stucco, thatch roof buildings, all attractively laid out with trees, lawns and tables. I learned that night that the grass was "mowed" by a small herd of springbok grazing in peace and safety.

Before we settled down to rest, bathe, or watch satellite TV, Peter made the rounds to make sure everyone was okay. I commented on how thoughtful the hotel staff were to leave a little wiener-shaped sand bag in front of each door in case a sudden downpour caused the water to rise over the sill. "Close, but no cigar," he said. "Be sure to keep it there, especially at night. It's to keep snakes and insects out." He added, gratuitously, with the smothered smile that I had come to know, "They're all *very* poisonous." And, he added that if I wanted to see the lions fed, I should be in the lobby at five.

Only the dashingly handsome Paul Newman-type and I went to see the lions. The enclosure into which we crept as though we were crawling through a tunnel was made of wood and had slits to peer out of. It seemed sturdy enough, but frankly it was reassuring to see several electrified wires outside. A gigantic, fully-maned lion appeared from nowhere dragging what looked like the hindquarter of some large animal. That's exactly what it was. He dropped it, looked around, snarled, then noisily ripped, chomped and growled meanly as a female came over. The enclosure was littered with bones bigger than my arm. I wasn't sure how I liked all this, but the guide whispered that both of the lions had been wounded and that the hotel had rescued them and brought them here for the "education" of the tourists.

We met by the pool for a swim and cocktails and were told to be back by 7:30 for dinner. Nearby, the hotel had enlarged a huge watering hole for the benefit of the guests as well as the animals. I wandered over to check it out before dinner because that was where "the big show" was to be later. As I approached I could see several Chapman's zebras drinking as one of their kind stood on the lookout. Together they retreated into the scrubby bushes and up over a small rise on the opposite edge of the small pond.

The observation side of the pit was lined with benches on a small bluff behind a fence. Under the fence were a maze of shrubs and snarls of barbed wire in case some agile something decided to have a few humans for supper.

About 6:40 the first jackal warily slunk down to the edge and took a discreet drink. It drank and left. At almost seven another jackal appeared, and then another. Gradually, as the sun set, there was a build-up of moderately noisy birds in the trees and bushes. People gently arrived to watch, and others left, but nobody said an audible word. It was amazing to hear only the bird calls.

A good-size fluffy white bird with feather pantaloons, a long black tail and a thick orangish curved beak landed on the bench next to me. I sat frozen still. Not even my eyes moved as it took note of me and then flew off. The Mokuti Lodge, as this oasis was called, had provided us with a very long list of birds that lived in this area, but my list was back at my room; and besides, I didn't care about the names as much as I did about memorizing the sights and sounds.

Time came for me to leave for dinner and I walked back across the trimmed green lawns. I passed the campground area with its dome tents and bunches of dedicated young white explorers and conservationist types sitting with their backs against the Jeeps, Land Rovers or VW buses, drinking beer or jugs of wine and stirring pots of something on the Coleman stoves. I could have been just as comfortable there and flashed on a time forty years ago when I had camped like that in every state and national park in Florida.

The dinner buffet was an artful masterpiece, and tall white chef's hats adorned the large smiling black men who carved thick slabs of rare roast beef, leg of lamb and several kinds of poultry. Numerous attractive black waitresses with the shiny black braids moved gracefully from table to table. There were expensive, elegant floral pieces everywhere. I realized that I hadn't seen one black tourist since we left Windhoek. Not all that long ago there were *no* white people here, and I began to think about the Pan African Union, which would like to have things that way again. Africa for the Africans. I thought about the WorldTeach volunteers in the Caprivi and along the Angolan border, where the bulk of the Namibian population, various black tribes, live. They were strong in traditional values but poor and illiterate about things that could improve their lives in a world that had been interrupted by invaders of all colors and types. The Angolan struggles were mixed with great intrigue and mystery beyond the scope of my understanding. Perhaps Peter had read my face or my thoughts, because he asked softly if I would like to share a bottle of wine. But of course, I said. "Tell me about Angola." "Maybe later," he said and ordered the wine. With all that wonderful food, he ate the same damn thing. Black bread, the smoked meat and a little potato salad.

I went back to the watering hole, with long pants, bug repellent and my grandfather's silver flask full of White Horse scotch. The sun was long gone, and the bright lights shining out away from the semi-circle of visitors had been on since dusk and didn't seem to bother the few animals that timidly crept to the water's edge. The audience was quieter than any church I had ever been in. Now the animals would come.

I found an empty cement bench at the far end of the railing. It was still hot to the touch. A sexy young couple emerged from the dark and quietly sat near me on the bench. His beefy hand slipped up and down her slender leg as she quietly rustled her cascade of red curls. Clearly he hadn't shaved all day. They whispered silently, and then he cupped his hands over his nose and mouth to squelch a sneeze. They quickly got up and left.

Another jackal trotted down from nowhere, sipped and then disappeared. A large cat appeared over the edge of the distant hill but then retreated. I guess it was understood among the animals that it was not "cricket" to catch your dinner at the drinking place, although what happens after a creature has drunk its fill and retreated I can only guess. Occasionally the darkness was pierced with a loud animal scream.

The night was pure black with truly diamond-brilliant stars.

A pleasant cool breeze washed over everything. People came and went, but in total silence. It was wonderful. I sat quietly for a long time.

"Paul Newman" and his wife came up behind my bench. I invited them to sit down because, I whispered, "at 9:30 Peter is going to come crashing through the bushes in a tutu of ostrich feathers." I shouldn't have said that. They quickly left choking back chuckles. Minutes later Peter showed up with a frown and a beer, but then pointed as a Mother rhino and her baby approached the water.

It was so peaceful, the gentle breeze, the quiet. Everyone was quiet. People even walked reverently. So much was a religious experience of the true kind.

CHAPTER 12

SOUND WAVES

I think part of why I want to do radio is that people around the world need to be flooded with images and sounds of truth about the commonness of man. For reasons I don't fully understand, I had to come here to learn of my own legacy of strengthening the role of women in producing permanent peace.

From week seven, the Namib

With the drastic change in government, the new South Africa had a rare opportunity to change its radio and television services. All communications industries had just been deregulated. According to everyone I talked with, prior to deregulation all broadcast media had been state owned by SABC, the South Africa Broadcasting Corporation, a white-dominated and, I gather, a very bureaucratic organization. Individual creativity was pretty much suppressed, and everything was in English or Afrikaans except for a few small African-language stations that the government promoted as a part of apartheid. During my stay, things changed drastically from week to week, usually for the better, although dealing with eleven official languages created many nightmares for producers.

When I arrived in Cape Town in October I fished around on my little radio and found a variety of stations ranging from hip-hop to call-in talk shows and just about everything in between. A number of stations heard in Cape Town were based or programmed in Johannesburg or Durban.

I had set the morning wake-up to a station that I enjoyed because of its interesting mix of jazz and classics. But early the next morning I was awakened by "...*clap, clap, clap*...Deep in the heart of Texas" followed by a very cheery Doris Day song.

Still bleary I called the station and said, "Where do you *get* this stuff?" It was the beginning of a beautiful friendship with Damon Durant, studio manager and morning drive-time DJ for Fine Music Radio (FMR 101.3 MHz). FMR had done a great deal of audience research and, according to Durant, there was a strong desire among the morning drive commuters for that "upbeat old-timey, Doris Day, Deep in the Heart of Texas-type stuff." He invited me to come visit the station, which I did. It was located in a wonderful old brick warehouse just down the hill from my flat in Tamboeskloff. The building, known as Longkloof Studios, was being restored and converted into television and radio stations, recording studios, mixing studios, a sound stage, headquarters for news wire services and a number of publicity and media oriented businesses, and a terrific restaurant and bar.

The station was only eight months old. When deregulation was to come about, the head of the Cape Town Symphony Orchestra and a private group called 6th Street Studios had perceived a niche for a station that specialized in jazz and classical music. The head of the symphony went to Australia and studied a station called, I think, 2MSB, a volunteer-run non-profit community radio station with a small paid staff, which has been running successfully for over twenty years. With minor modifications to meet local standards and needs, 2MSB became the model for FMR.

FMR had applied for a license from the IBA, the Independent Broadcast Authority, which was the radio and TV licensing arm of the new South African government created to implement the changes of all media. FMR had been granted a community license (not a commercial license) which meant, technically, they couldn't sell advertising. The criteria for a community radio station were that they had to be non-profit and controlled by the community. While some of the original money had come from the symphony and the 6th Street Studios, an astonishingly successful membership subscription drive and donations had brought in more money. It still wasn't quite enough to pay the bills in the beginning, so they were permitted to sell some advertising. After a one-year probationary license, performance was to be reviewed, they would be permitted to apply for a four-year license. Until they got their permanent license, they were renting equipment. As a non-profit organization, they would be able to buy excellent equipment, and they planned to do top-notch training.

Just before leaving the States for South Africa in October 1995, I heard a short interview with John Mattison, a journalist who used to work for our National Public Radio (NPR) in Johannesburg and was then a Counsellor of South Africa's Independent Broadcast Authority, the grantor of licenses. Our analog was the Federal Communications Commission, the FCC. He said that there were already about eighty community radio stations in South Africa, ranging in view from radical this to radical that. According to Mattison, the sheer number and diversity of radio stations permit exposition of various views and keep one point of view from dominating others, a theory that seemed to be working. For example, there were three stations in Soweto, directly serving perhaps three million people, but you also could pick up what could be called a white supremacist station and certainly a lot of what were known as "Jesus stations." Some of the religious stations advocated approaches that were contrary to a secular view of how to produce true well-being for black listeners. But that's free speech.

My interest in private non-commercial radio—community radio—had been increasing steadily over the years, not just because of much trivial and trash programming on commercial radio, but because of endless, mindless commercials. I had listened to community-type radio stations in Ecuador, Alaska and elsewhere and had written and produced three programs for the community radio station (KXCI) in Tucson. I still had much to learn, but I had a few things to contribute, so I hung around FMR quite a bit when I was in Cape Town. FMR was a very comfortable situation of give and take, the essence of real education—all teachers and all learners. I kept reflecting on the infancy of the new South Africa in which I found myself.

I recorded an interview with Damon shortly before leaving. He had a lot to say: "...The changes [in the communications industries] really cheesed off a lot of what I call the 'hoity-toity' colonialists, who thought they could keep everything their way. But change is necessary for the evolution of our own very unique culture.

"It has to happen. I think it is important that white people, including me, learn at least one black language, because then I could understand some of the very good programming that is being produced. I only speak English and Afrikaans, and I reckon that only ten percent of the white community understands a black language. We need to realize that we whites are only a small part of the community." He added wryly that if you really planned your TV viewing carefully, you could catch the top notch BBC programs.

Damon had been an intelligence officer in the South African army in Angola. Rashid Lombard, a photo-journalist and former ANC activist had also been in the war on the Angolan-Namibian border where, technically, they had been committed to killing each other. Now Rashid is executive manager of the station and Damon's immediate boss and good friend.

The former management of the government-owned radio stations, the conservative white-dominated South African Broadcasting Corporation, contended that black people didn't listen to classical music. FMR research found that over half their classical listenership was in the townships. Rashid, as a person of color who therefore had been raised in a township, said that his family listened to classics and opera all of the time. Rashid had an incredible record collection of all types of music, which he kept at the station for everyone's use to augment the growing permanent collection. And he also had taken the thirteen large portraits of famous African jazz musicians, which made up the 1995 Guinness calendar and which among other pictures, posters and notices, adorned the studio walls.

My TV viewing in southern Africa was confined, by choice, to the evening hours. There were lots of interesting nature programs, which people just ate up, well done locally produced programs, magazine shows, and programs like "60 Minutes." The weather—I should say the weather reporting—was unbelievably crude and dull, something that quickly changed when the TV system was dramatically overhauled while I was there.

The eight o'clock news, in English on one of the two channels and in Afrikaans on the other (unless you had additional
cable channels) was well enough done, and without the empha-
sis on hairdos, makeup and costume that we lavish on our own
airheads. But the news often was starkly realistic (as were the
color pictures on the front pages of papers), showing a murder
victim from every possible angle, including a picture from
inside the morgue.

I was watching a news story about the necessity of quelling a
demonstration in Namibia; with me were the two black nurses
who were attending some kind of meeting and staying at the
same pension as I was. We all winced as a cop methodically
slipped on black leather gloves and then, as several policemen
held down a demonstrator, the TV crew actually filmed him trying to gouge out a demonstrator's eyes with his gloved hands.
Unfortunately that sort of stuff was still very much a reality. I
thought of the Rodney King incident, which also was given
much play in South Africa.

There were quite a few cleverly produced segments about
how the government worked, the legislative process or even how
to mark a ballot and the importance of voting. It seemed very
elemental until I reminded myself that most of the people in the
country had never voted before.

CNN, MTV and other TV channels could be seen if you had
cable, but most people didn't have it. I noticed that in a number
of restaurants at noon the TV would be tuned to Larry King and
CNN news—with an attentive audience watching.

Television as well as radio was controlled by SABC—now a
much changed SABC. On February 8, 1996, the two television
channels of SABC changed to three channels. Instead of using
just English and Afrikaans, most of the eleven official languages
were now used at some time during the week, although several
related languages were grouped together, because speakers of
certain African languages could understand several others. Ngu-
ni and Sotho were grouped. Xhosa and Zulu were grouped.
Many blacks and almost all whites speak English and Afrikaans.

The three-hour-long flashy inauguration ceremony for the
new SABC took place at an airforce base near Pretoria and used
a huge South African Airways plane as a prop. President

171

Mandela, the white woman head of the new Broadcast Corporation, and other dignitaries emerged from the plane and made speeches, followed by a parade of black celebrities, including Stevie Wonder, a triumphant Johnny Cochran, who had just finished the Simpson trial, and other famous Afro-American "stars," none of whom I had ever heard of. There was much staging, laser lights, music, dancing, etc. But the best part for me, as always, was the African drummers. I had never heard anything resembling that kind of rhythm and music, even on records. Incredible.

People explained how the new channels would work, but for weeks it was fascinating trying to find news in English. On the street, people cursed the changes and everyone complained about not being able to find anything in their own language. The three South African Broadcasting Corporation channels wrestled mightily with mixing the programming, and gradually things got better and people could find enough of what they wanted.

I kept reflecting on what a momentous few months I had witnessed and how fortunate I was to just happen to be there. There were rugby championships, soccer championships, and in November South Africa got full satellite transmission. The first local elections were held everywhere (except in recalcitrant KwaZulu Natal). The draft constitution was moving toward ratification, and there were many other first-time experiences for all of us. I actually felt very patriotic for South Africa and joyous about the future of the country. It was all so swift and amazing.

Another first and important thing that was happening in South Africa was the manufacture of the BayGen Radio, a portable radio about a foot long, a foot high and six inches deep that is powered by the newly patented Baylis wind-up generator. Sixty cranks on the handle lasted for about forty, clear, "as-loud-as-you-want" minutes of A.M., F.M. or short wave.

Radio had, since its inception, been of importance to those living in remote areas. Eskimos and farmers got weather information, religious stations spread the word to those in the hinterlands. Information could be spread to those who would otherwise have little contact with the outside world.

Lack of electricity and the cost of batteries had been a problem, especially in poor areas. Of increasing importance was the contamination caused by the disposal of large numbers of batteries.

The first licensed use of this unique wind-up generator was the BayGen freeplay radio—manufactured in Cape Town. It wasn't commercially available yet, and it was my understanding that the manufacturers wanted first needs to be filled first—poor and rural parts of the world first. Hooray for them, I say. I was permitted to buy one to bring back because the first words out of my mouth were "I'm working with community radio," not "I want the franchise."

In a township I visited a "station" that operated only when they had electricity and someone to make announcements. It also was a source of recipes and nutritional information, political announcements, music and medical information and a chance for citizens of the desperately poor neighborhood to express their views. That station consisted of a microphone and a control board in a very old trailer with a small antenna and a signal only strong enough to reach those in the immediate area. The potential of the BayGen radio in situations like this was self-evident.

The importance of community radio was recognized in the New South Africa as cheap, immediately accessible and taking advantage of the "oral tradition," especially important in communities where large numbers of people were illiterate. The customary means of passing on history, tradition and information remains the spoken word. The problem of illiteracy itself was being helped with the aid of radio.

Reading, writing, critical thinking *and* understanding the spoken word are what will make or break us.